From A Victim

to

A Voice

Overcoming Domestic Violence

To my new
a good friend
Bettye mcgiee
Carolyn W Love Hunter

Carolyn Washington - Hunter

From a Victim to A Voice

© 2018 Carolyn Washington-Hunter

Printed in the USA

ISBN (Print Version): ISBN- 978-1798413807

Cover: Shekinah Glory Publishing

Publisher: Shekinah Glory Publishing

Dedication

This book is dedicated to every woman who has Broken her silence like Mariechelle Malveaux, and to women who have not found the courage to do so yet.

We stand for you, and to all those who have lost their fight in or to Domestic Violence… I say I haven't forgot about you, but I remember and salute you on this day!

Carolyn Washington-Hunter

Acknowledgements

Our Heavenly Father God, who made all this possible.

My mother…Ruby Washington.

My husband…Wendell Hunter.

My children… Aliyah Bonner, Laila Smith, Kirklin Bonner

My employer,

My Bishop…Eddie Ferguson

My Publishing Company…Shekinah Glory Publishing

Nicole Highsmith

Linda Rowe

Ron Lewis

My dear friend…Janice Johns, one of the few who I would often cry around, and she would tell me God was going to bring me out.

Thank you to each one of you for your love, support and kindness. Because of you I was able to keep going and make it through that trying period of my life

Table of Contents

Introduction

"The School of Pain"

We live in a world that is filled with a wealth of delusion. The world has created platforms that would cause you to think that everything in life is perfect and whole. Well, I beg to differ, because there are people every day who are experiencing various forms of hurt and pain. There are people who wear masks to hide the truth behind their brokenness, because of the shame associated with their pain. I to was one on those people who learned how to mask the pain and torment that my soul was experiencing on a daily basis. When people looked at me on the outside, they couldn't see the little girl in me who was molested and violated for years. When people see me, they can't tell that I once lived a life full of self-sabotage.

There is no way, they could see it, because I wasn't going to allow it to be revealed. I had too many dirty secrets to keep buried in the depths of my soul, but one day God said, no more! It dawned on me that I wasn't moving forward, and my unhealthy decisions were my fault. Yes, I was violated in many ways, but I still was, and currently is, in control of my life. You see what I didn't realize then, that I know now, is that Carolyn, was on the front row in the school of life. Life was teaching me some valuable lessons and I had to choose to pay attention, take notes, and be prepared to ace my life tests so that I could be elevated.

Let me share some wisdom with you! Pain is a motivator! Pain will motivate you to do things you wouldn't dream of. Pain is a great teacher, when we allow ourselves to listen and learn. Pain is used by God to elevate us to greater levels. You see most people become common with their comfort zones and refuse to endure process. We were never created to remain in one place. You see this just with age. Each year we grow older, bigger, and wiser. Pain pushes us to be great, when we allow it. As you prepare to read through the pages of this book, you will encounter a wealth of pain on almost every page. I would like for you to keep in mind, that you are reading this book because I allowed the pain to be a motivator and elevator for me.

Enduring abuse at the hands of people you trust is not easy to digest, but no matter what, the lessons I learned along the journey of my life have been valuable. The wisdom I now have is priceless and what the enemy tried to do, which was take my life and stop my purpose, didn't work. I pressed through the pain and I survived. Yes, I survived. I can't begin to tell you how I made it, but it was through the power of God and faith. You can't see the miracle manifesting, you just have to believe that God is faithful and be willing to wait on Him to deliver. I suffered at the hands of many people because I wasn't secure within myself. Take a long hard look at my life. As you turn the pages, seek to look beyond the black words on the white sheets of paper. Dig deep within your soul and allow yourself to become one with my story. If you are not in an abusive relationship, you could very well know someone who is. Take the time to reflect and understand what a person truly goes through from a mental standpoint when they are in this position. Don't be so quick to judge the matter. Don't be so quick to say this will never be me. I never saw it for my life and I'm sure many others didn't see it either. My desire through this book is to save as many people as I can from repeating the same dysfunctional, unhealthy and detrimental mistakes that I made by looking for love in all the wrong places and trying to force someone to be a bandage for my pain. This only caused deeper wounds and more inward bleeding. As you take this journey with me, buckle your seat beat and prepare for a bumpy ride, that will smooth out towards the end to a life filled with victory. Remember, be a voice and not a victim!

Carolyn Washington-Hunter

Chapter One

"Shattered Innocence"

My story begins as a little girl, who overtime developed into a broken woman. I was born into a very large family. My father birth five children with his first wife. Then he married my mother who had five children prior to their union, and together they birth an additional six children. Then he fathered two more children, making the grand total, seventeen children in all. As a young girl, I witnessed and heard more than any child should be allowed to hear or see. I was subjected to things that would cause me to shift from a bubbly little girl into an introverted being with a deep dark secret. A secret that would equate to hiding an ugly scar. Something no one could ever see or know that I was experiencing. Something that I could hide in plain sight. To be honest it was very easy to hide amid all those siblings because everyone had their own issues going on.

I was an innocent little girl who was focused on the simple things in life, such as playing with dolls, coloring and having fun. One day, my focus shifted, after being approached by one of the males in my family. It wasn't an innocent touch. It was a touch that would lead to my innocence being stolen from me. A touch that would create a domino effect of molestation and rape. A brutal violation that began and seemed as though it would never end. The ironic thing is, this wasn't just one male family member, but two and these males were my older brothers. Quite naturally I was told by my offenders not to tell because I could get them sent away and in a lot of trouble. I was four years old. How was I supposed to process this at such a young age? How do you violate someone and then make them feel guilty or try to convince them not to violate you back? During these heinous acts I would find myself staring at the ceiling, trying to manipulate my mind to be anywhere, but in that moment of being raped. During this time, we lived in Nacogdoches, Texas, right in front of a railroad track. There was a creek that ran along the side of our house. My favorite place was the backyard. There was a fig tree that was just low enough for me to sit in and eat figs.

My mother would often leave me at home as she visited friends and neighbors. I would beg her to please take me with her, but she often refused and said she would be back later. As soon as the door closed, I knew I was in trouble. I can remember one particular day when she was leaving. I tried to run out of the house behind her, but I made it as far as the front door, before being dragged back into the bedroom and raped again, and again, and again. Let me repeat, I was only four years old. My little body experiencing things that my mind could neither fathom or even understand. There came a point when I thought the attacks would end because my mother enrolled me into pre-kindergarten. I was very excited, because though very young, I had enough sense to know that being at school, would eliminate most of my time at home.

I started school and I will never forget one of my classmates who would take her pencil and sexually motion it between her legs while sitting in her desk. I could relate to what she was doing, because of what I was experiencing at home. I was raped until the tender age of six when we moved to Hitchcock, Texas. I was glad to finally be away from the perpetrators, but let's be honest, my body was in a new location, but the thoughts and the visuals remained.

Each year as I grew older, the anger within evolved as well. I tried to confide in an older family member, also my brother, but he turned on me and tried to sexually abuse me as well. This left me empty and lifeless. I had to carry this pain all by myself. Who could I trust? Why was this happening to me? No matter what, I silently carried the guilt and shame as if I did something wrong. I chose never to tell anyone anything else again. I didn't care if it was good or bad. I learned early in life not to trust people and to fend for myself. People say "you can talk to me" or "you can trust me" but quickly change or betray each other's trust. At some point I started spiraling out of control. I started searching for coping mechanisms. I became involved in drinking at an early age. My mother had her hands full with the older siblings who were getting in trouble. They were going in and out of jail, so she didn't notice her baby girl slipping away into a deep dark place by the age of eleven.

We grew up in a small town, therefore no one ever questioned my age because I was developed in areas that a grown woman would be. My family was well known; therefore no one questioned my age. I joined my siblings in the night club life, where I continued to drink and became very promiscuous. I started being taken advantage of sexually at a young age. This caused me to become confused as to what love really was. I thought sex was an expression of love, because every time I was raped, I was asked afterwards do you love me. Then I was told, if you love me don't tell. They said it and I listened, but I didn't know there was a difference between the two. I also didn't know that God had a plan for my life and truly loved me even though I was enduring these horrible tragedies. I built a wall around myself. If you didn't bother me, I wasn't going to bother you. Now, if you crossed the line or climbed over the wall, then you were going to see a side of me that wasn't too pleasant.

I remember being in the 8th grade and one of my friends had a fight with a young lady. So, I decided I was going to get my part in and let her know not to mess with me or my people. After the fight the young lady was sitting on the floor crying. I walked up behind her, reached into my pocket and pulled out a lighter. I set the girls hair on fire. I'm not bragging or boasting about any of this, but I want you to know how troubled I was as a young person, whose life had been turned upside down. I was willing to make others hurt the way I was hurting. Have you ever heard the expression "hurt people hurt people"? Well I was living that repeatedly, not realizing the damage I was causing to others or myself because of the damage that had been done to me. You see I carried a razor blade between my fingers, one in my hair, and I kept knives on my waistline. I stayed ready for anything. The coach of the class frantically ran over putting the fire out, then escorting the young lady and my friend who had the fight to the principal's office. I sat on the bleachers as if I had not done anything, however minutes later the principal came to escort me to the office where there was a uniformed officer waiting for me. He instructed me to turn around and put my hands behind my back. He handcuffed me and my friend and drove us down to the local police department in Hitchcock, Texas. We sat there waiting to be transferred to the county, due to the seriousness of the crime. The officer arrived from Galveston County and shackled me like I was an animal. He put chains on my feet, which connected to a belt around my waist; and my wrist were cuffed to the waist belt as he led us to the back seat of an unmarked police car. As we were driving, I looked out the window and saw my mom in the passenger seat of a car driving by. A family friend or someone had gotten word to her that I was in trouble. We didn't have a home phone back in those days. In that very moment it was as if God allowed time to stop. As the cars passed our eyes landed directly on each other and I could see the pain, hurt, confusion and disappointment in her eyes. I instantly felt bad because I wasn't trying to cause my mother any more pain. The car my mother was in immediately turned around and started following us.

Not knowing the magnitude of the crime, I had just committed·I was under the assumption that I was going to be released and sent home with my mom. I told the officer that my mother was following behind us and that she would follow us wherever we go. He pulled over, as did the driver of the car my mother was in. He walked to the car to speak with my mother and when I looked back the car was driving off in the opposite direction. I was looking back in total confusion wondering where my mother was going. Why wasn't she following me to take me home? When the officer came back, he explained that my mother would have to come to my arraignment.

Now it was starting to settle in that I was in big trouble. I would like to encourage young boys and girls to watch who they call friends, because it is very easy to get tied up in things that have nothing to do with them. It is very easy to become guilty by association.

Since my friend was loyal and wouldn't tell on me, she went down with me. She was completely innocent except for the fist fight she was involved in. Once we made it to the facility, I was given specific instructions on what to do. I was fingerprinted and escorted to the back separating me from my friend. I was given a uniform to put on and a tube of chemicals to put in my hair in case I received a roommate. This was for the prevention of lice per the female officer.

Well those chemicals messed my cute jerry curl up. The officer watched as I showered then escorted me to my cell. The door slammed so hard it seems as if I can still hear it slamming today after all these years and the cell was extremely cold. The cell had a commode with a bed that looked like a bath-tube that had been filled with cement and a mat about two inches thick. This was not what I intended for my life, but I made a choice that wasn't a very good one. As I was standing in the cold cell, there was a bible on the floor. I instantly began to weep and plead with God to get me out of my situation. I promised to serve Him, if he delivered me out of this one.

The next morning, I went before the judge. My mother and father were there and thankfully I could go home under strict circumstances with my parents. After getting home my mother told me to stay out of trouble as we were waiting on my trial date to come around. My charge was 25 years aggravated assault. It didn't look good for me because the state had witnesses and signed statements against me, therefore I was guilty as charged. But I had a praying mother and a big GOD.

Well I didn't stop there, I had a disagreement with one of my brothers after being released. It was around the Thanksgiving holiday because I remember being in our dining room standing in front of the gas heater trying to warm myself. For no apparent reason he stood in my face yelling rather loudly. So, I picked up a knife off the table, stuck it in the fire and when he opened his mouth again, I stabbed him in the chest. I'm not making any excuses, but when you have been victimized, you tend to fight back by any means necessary. My brother was flown by life flight to UTMB hospital in Galveston. I am happy to report he survived the attack and is still living today. A few days later a detective showed up to talk with my mother. He said, "Your daughter has set a girl on fire and we know she stabbed your son. She is a menace to society, and we need to get her off the street before she kills someone."

My mother was heartbroken, but she was a praying woman. As time progressed and I waited for my day in court and my fate to be decided I received a letter in the mail from the District Attorney's office (DA's) of Galveston County. The letter said any and all charges had been dropped against me. The state decided not to proceed with the case. At that point I knew only GOD could make this happen. But, to be perfectly honest I just wanted God to get me out of trouble. I didn't have any intentions on serving Him. I just needed His help at that moment and made a quick promise to serve Him.

Shame on me, but we as people do this all the time. Get me out Jesus! Get me out fast! And as soon as He does, that's all we really wanted, then we are back to business as usual with no change in our lives. Oh, but God had a plan and purpose for my life even though I couldn't see or know it yet. Mother's, Aunt's, Grandmothers families please listen to your daughters cry when she is speaking to you without saying words through tears, violence, and attitudes. She's asking, for help; as I was but didn't know how. So, I drank and did any and everything I felt I was big and bad enough to do. I went to school, but I made sure I had my happy juice (alcohol beverage) before I went. I stayed intoxicated all while smiling at my mom like I was a little angel. I can remember being suspended week after week. I became my own worst enemy because it was my way or no way. While I was acting a donkey being sent home from school, life was still going on. My classmates were advancing classes and grade levels while I was still a freshman. I always seemed to get myself in some type of bind. I can remember being at a man's house where I had no business being. I told him I was thirsty, and we had already been drinking alcoholic beverages earlier that day.

He bought me some apple juice, but as I was drinking, I looked into the bottom of the glass and saw something fizzing like an Alka-Seltzer. The next thing I remember was waking up at home in my bed the next day. I didn't know how I got there. I got up looking around and found my clothes from the night before with mud on the pants. I had some suede low purple heels, but I only had one shoe. I didn't understand so I asked my mother some questions not to give away where I had been or up to because I didn't want to worry her. My mother explained she heard a loud bang on our front door around 2:00a.m., she said she opened the front door and I fell in. She said she managed to put me on the couch and from time to time she said she would get up to check on me. The last time she said she got up I was gone from the couch and she found me in my bed. I don't remember any of that still to this day, but I do remember feeling different in my body like something had happened to me that morning after waking up. I never told my mother anything about that night. Today I can remember bits and pieces, but not everything. However, I did finally tell my mom that I was raped as a little girl. She started crying and saying, "oh my baby" as we talked for hours. I know that I didn't tell her out of fear, but after witnessing her disheartening reaction I only wished I would have told her sooner. I assured her during the conversation that I was alright because I fought through. What was meant to break me, though drastic, only made me fight to live and become stronger. During our conversation my mother revealed to me that she was also raped, which led to the pregnancy of my older brother. Then she told me that my sister had been raped and at that point I just felt numb. To think that I was an innocent child born into a generational cycle of sexual perversion was unreal. This made me loathe having girls in the event that God blessed me with children because there was no way I wanted my daughter to experience this foolishness. It just makes me think we must do better as families not to keep secrets, because had I known just think I may have had the courage to come forward sooner.

BE A VOICE NOT A VICTIM!

Chapter Two

"Dysfunctional Distractions"

As time went on, I didn't graduate with my class because I couldn't pass the math part of the TAAS test. I was totally crushed, however, I started living what I thought was my best life. After all the hell I put my mother through we moved to Texas City, Texas right in front of a Pentecostal Church called Macedonia Pentecostal Church. It has now been renamed Macedonia Ministries. This is where my life forever changed. The God, I had been asking to watch over me, protect me, and keep me out of trouble showed up. I was 18 years old now and began to focus on learning who God was and what the bible teaches us as Christians.

It wasn't long before I became distracted. I met this guy who caught my attention and it wasn't long before I stopped going to church. Well, this was a horrible mistake. He lived in Houston, Texas and it didn't take long for him to reveal his other side. You know that side that doesn't appear when you first meet a person. He was very abusive, both verbally and physically. He would slap me around and drag me through his mother's house. Yes, I said, his mothers house. That should have been red flag number one, but I was still young and learning the do's and don'ts of life. There were times when I felt like he was Ike and I was Tina; the abuse was so bad. I can't begin to tell you how embarrassed I was. He had no respect for me, nor did I have very much for myself to be tolerating the abuse. But this is what looking for love looks like when you have no clue what you are looking for. The years of sexual abuse I endured and the physical abuse I witnessed painted a picture in my mind that this was normal, therefore I didn't share the experiences with anyone. I knew in the inner most depths of my heart that I had to get away from this man. I started praying and asking God to provide a way of escape. I promised Him that I would return home if He just got me out of this situation.

Well, God was merciful, and it felt like God just opened the door and I ran with all my heart, might and soul. I ran back to my mother's house and I found myself on my knees at the altar asking God to forgive and save me. This was just the beginning. I went back to church and began to seek God with my whole heart. Well, the enemy is always seeking to kill, steal and destroy when you find yourself on a path for God. Therefore, I will say again, watch who you call friends. They can mean you good but cause so much trouble or damage just by their words.

I met another man at the grocery store. Everything in me said no this isn't for you. He gave me his number and I went about my business shoving the number in my purse. I talked with my friend about the young man a few days later and she started giving me her advice. She began down talking me, saying I was so boring because all I did was go to church. She criticized the way I dressed and said I had no life and I would never meet anyone. Those words rang in my head and were hurtful coming from a person I trusted as a sister in Christ. I began to feel low and hearing the words of my friend needless to say, I called the guy. Let me be very honest. I knew from the beginning that he had some screws loose, but I wasn't willing to be alone. There I was, tangled in another dysfunctional relationship.

This was my first run in that I knew of with a narcissistic individual. He was very controlling and before I knew it, I was moving to Houston into an apartment with this young man. He turned out to be an abusive liar and thief, but I was in love or so I thought. I didn't even know him or anything concerning him. I only knew what he said to me and of course I ate every word of it up true or not. We as women must take the time to do research and investigate the truth. We can't take what these men say at face value and just run with it. Let's be honest, I didn't have any idea of what love really was or felt like. It didn't take long for me to feel like I was going to lose my mind.

He played a lot of mind games with me making me feel I was never good enough. At this point I'm 19 years old and he was 25. I'm sure he was thinking what a young stupid puppet he had on his hands. I convinced myself he was from God because I had been praying, fasting, and sending my offerings to church. I was going to church here and there when I felt like it, and this man seem to say all the right things at the right time. So, I was thinking this is it, he is the one. I wasn't even close to finding the one, because the one I needed to find first and foremost was me. Not only was he a liar, cheater and con artist, but he lived a double life. He loved the ladies! Eventually he began talking to me about moving in together, however, the reality was he needed me to move so he could move in with me and out of his mother's home. He lived with his mother, but he made it sound as if he allowed his mother to live with him and he was taking care of her. I found myself entangled in another web of dysfunction.

The lease, lights, and home phone were all in my name. He even convinced me to get him a vehicle and yes, I did in my name. I was caught up again in this foolishness looking for love. It didn't take long for his true identity to show up. We moved together in late July and by September everything was coming out the closet and into the light.

People can only pretend to be someone for so long and then their true identity will manifest.

During this time, I was working as a home health aide. I had one private self-pay client and I cleaned homes. Yes, I had three jobs and would be exhausted all the time. One day I decided to stop at the apartment before going to my next job. Well he was home with his feet kicked up on the coffee table playing the PlayStation. I was as shocked to catch him home as he was at me that I had come home to take a break during work hours. The nerve of me, right? After a brief conversation I found out he had been getting dressed every morning and leaving the apartment saying he was on his way to work. Well he was doubling back once I left for work and then leaving before I got home in the evening. Truth be told he didn't have a job at all. He swore he had a job lined up and would start working soon. It was some collection agency on the Southwest side of Houston. I have always paid my bills on time, so I kept up with them. My jobs paid me the same amount weekly. I didn't spend money on myself, so even if I wasn't writing it down, I still knew what was in my bank account. However, he didn't know that. I was sitting at home at the dining room table one afternoon when he calls me out of the blue asking was everything ok? Did I need anything? I responded no, to not needing anything and hung up the phone. Not even thirty minutes later boom the power goes off, yes, the lights were turned off. I called him back immediately and his response was okay I will take care of it. He asked me if there was anything else while rushing me off the phone at the same time as if I was bothering him. Well now I'm curious because I'm thinking in my mind, he has no money, so I checked my purse and my bank card was gone. Now I'm in deep thought about all the fishy things I've been witnessing. He was giving me money to get my nails done, taking me shopping, but turns out it was with my own money. Talk about trifling! He was handing me my own money and with a straight face.

He was sneaking my bank card out of my purse and withdrawing money, then putting it back as if the money came from him before I missed or noticed it. When I would check the mailbox, there were never any bills coming. One day I got up and headed straight to the bank. I cancelled that bank card and saw all the charges where he was using my hard-earned money to buy and entertain others. Not shortly after that I can remember standing outside at his truck one afternoon talking to him when I noticed a small compartment on the passenger side. It wasn't closed all the way and I could see some type of papers hanging out. Quickly I turned my head as not to give away what I was looking at. Later that night once he was asleep, I made my way down to the truck to see what was in the compartment. All the bills that had been coming in he had intercepted them and hid them in this compartment of the truck. I also found pictures of different women.

I was crushed to say the least. My heart was broken again by another man taking advantage of me and calling it love. It got to the point where I couldn't sleep. He started coming in later and later, as if he didn't care about me or the dysfunctional relationship, we were in. Apparently, he was coming in late from his new job. We became strangers living in the same space and I didn't know about him, but I was very unhappy.

I called my Pastor at that time and told him what was going on in my life and he gave me counsel over the phone. He said if you want God to move then you need to move and right now. He asked me if there was someone I could stay with. I packed some clothes and went to stay with my aunt without telling her what was going on in my personal life. However, through the day I would stop by the apartment because I still worked in the area. Being a woman, I would look for clues, answers, anything that would make sense because he wasn't telling me anything. I checked through the Caller Id writing every name and number down that I didn't know. So, after about a week I came to the apartment one night around 9:00pm and I called him saying guess where I am? I tell you he must have flew home in a spaceship running up the stairs. He asked me why I was there and how long I had been there. Then he had the nerves to ask me to go downstairs to get his cigarettes. I politely looked at him and smiled and said I don't smoke, get them yourself.

I could tell something wasn't right and he was up to something or hiding something. He took off running down the stairs to retrieve them but not fast enough. The telephone rang and of course I answered it. It was a female on the other line looking for him. I recognized the number as one I had written down. I asked who she was and told her who I was. She apologized saying he told her he lived with his cousin and didn't know he had a girlfriend living with him. I suggested she could call back in a few minutes and he would answer. I hung up and sat on the arm of my crème color sectional sofa. He come through the door in a hurry and I didn't say anything at that moment. The phone started ringing. He looked at me and I said to him answer it, it's for you. I have already spoken with her. He ran to turn the answering machine off and then yanked the phone cord from the wall. Apparently, he was experiencing loss of hearing, so I repeated myself. I already talked to her! I said it for the second time. He heard me because he charged towards me knocking me off the sofa by punching me in the mouth. I was totally baffled, enraged, but again just numb. He hit me so hard he busted my lip. Then he started apologizing while at the same time saying it was my fault and that he needed time to cool off. He suggested that I leave. Despite this abusive incident, the lies and the women I was still holding on to him in my heart. I left in tears but the rejected little girl on the inside of me was longing for him and would call him repeatedly. No matter what he wouldn't answer. I would go by there and find that he was out for the night enjoying his life with someone else, while I was left with a lot of pain and betrayal. It was becoming apparent that men could hurt you and just go on with their lives as if nothing happened. This was starting to become an ongoing trend in my life. It didn't dawn on me that I was just being used and taken advantage of.

One day he finally decided to inform me that he would be moving out to get some space. He tried to play me by saying we would eventually get back together as a couple, but he needed to do this first. Also, he was going to help me (lol) yes help me with the bills. He planned to take certain items out of the house, including the truck that was in my name. I said okay still holding on to hope and what I thought was love. It took no time at all for him to forget about me. He moved on with his life, while I was still licking my wounds and not willing to let go of what had let go of me a long time ago. Not long after I received a certified letter from the company that financed the truck. I was approaching three months past due. I reached out to him to inform him that I needed help paying the bills he left me with. He had a new job selling cars, but couldn't pay for his truck, how ironic. I didn't tell him that I received the letter from the finance company. I borrowed a friend's car so I could drive to his job.

I called one of my brothers to ride with me. The wrong brother I might add, in order to drive the other truck back and not to mention it was a standard shift (stick) which he never taught me how to drive. He promised to teach me upon signing for it, but never got around to it. He told me to meet him on Saturday at his job and he would give me some money to help me, I drove up to his job while waiting on him to show up he was on a test drive with a customer. I found myself waiting with another lady who had just walked up, and we began to converse casually when I found out she was waiting for him as well. She told me to let him know she stopped by in a sarcastic tone. I continued to wait then finally he showed up. He gave me $250 cash. I took the money and put it in the vehicle I was driving.

I walked back over to him saying, I need to talk to you. I informed him I wanted my truck and I knew he had not been paying the payments and to give it to me or I would call the police. He started yelling and calling me all kinds of nasty-names talking to me as if I was a prostitute who he had picked up off the streets. He was helping me to get my life in order in front of all the customers and employees. He ran to the truck and began to rip things out of the truck such as the radio and speakers I had put in for him. Talk about petty! One of his coworkers came over saying you guys are making a scene, stop it the police are on their way. He and I pushed each other back and forward then he spit in my face. Yes, the ultimate form of disrespect. He started calling me more horrible names when he suddenly remembered he had just given me money and told me to give it back.

Of course, I said no, he started running over to the vehicle I drove to his job. I yelled to my brother to lock the doors as he ran toward the truck and I followed behind him. He went to the driver side pulling at the handle and it was locked, then he went around to the passenger side where my brother was sitting. My brother had the window cracked enough for him to put his hand inside the vehicle. He stuck his hand in reaching for the lock and I put my hand in the window fighting him to get his hand out and off the vehicle. Well my brother did nothing to help me at all. The police arrived on the scene and he quickly headed over to the officer to give his side of the story. He said I was an ex-girlfriend who he was no longer with and I came to his job harassing him. The officer was very rude to me as he believed his story. The officer said, "How are you going to drive two vehicles?" I stood there crying and pointing over to the other vehicle and explained that my brother was the second driver. After confirming it was my vehicle, I was given minutes to exit the property.

Ladies I don't have to tell you the shame, humiliation, embarrassment, and anger I felt in that moment. I was furious with my brother for not helping me as this man threw me all over the parking lot, spat in my face, and belittled me in front of everyone. I thought to myself I wish I could leave him here, but I needed him to drive the truck.

Despite the pain and sheer humiliation, I managed to pick myself up and drive off the property with my head held high. Needless to say, I found myself in a very depressed state of being. I could hardly get out of bed. I called him up on the phone to tell him that he broke my heart and I wanted him to hear me die. He asked what I had done. I had taken a half bottle of pain killers. He started getting frantic and asking where I was. I told him I was at home. He called the paramedics, so I got into my vehicle and went down the street to a pay phone to call him back. I asked him why would he do that? He asked where I was again, and I told him. Once again, he informed 911 that I was at a gas station on Ellington Field. I hung up and drove down to Edgebrook Road. I called him back on another pay phone and he said Carolyn the paramedics can't keep chasing you around they have other emergencies. Then he followed up with he had to go because he had some where to be. I got back in my vehicle and cried. I drove to the AMC movie theatre on 45 and the Beltway. I sat in the parking lot crying to God asking Him why He wouldn't just let me die. At that moment I heard a still small voice say, "Not yet I have use for you!" I called my sister and dear friend from church, Alesia Horton to tell her what I had done. She met me at my apartment and stayed with me while I slept for three days. She never left my side. She continued to watch over me as I slept off the pain medication. Just think I really could have died and for what, a man who made it very clear that he didn't want me. It took some time, but finally realized that he wasn't coming back, and as much as it hurt, I had to move on.

At this point only God could intervene and stop the painful feelings I was experiencing. I was still deeply in love with this man, even after all that he had done. I know this sounds crazy, but we can't control who we think we love, and we definitely can't control them loving us back. As time went on, I couldn't afford the vehicle, so it was repossessed. I lost all my customers and clients because I couldn't get to work. I had to take a job working at a gas station making $7.25 an hour. I walked to and from work, still behind on bills, praying just to make it through the days feeling hurt, emotionally drained and wounded.

Chapter Three

"A Whirlwind of Abuse"

Now you would think that I wouldn't even want to see another guy, let alone get involved with one, but that wasn't my story. While I was working at the gas station, I met another guy who would frequent the station quite often. We developed a friendship and when he discovered I was walking to and from work, he started picking me up and dropping me off as a friendly jester. He did this for a while and eventually we grew closer. Well, I found myself confiding in him about my previous relationships. In my mind I was giving him fair warning of what I wasn't about to tolerate from another man. He told me he was interested in me, but I felt the need to give him step by step instructions of how I expected to be treated. I failed to do this in the other relationships. Maybe this time, I could get a different result if I asked for what I wanted and needed. I questioned whether God would allow me to endure the shame, hurt and embarrassment of another dysfunctional relationship. Well, the answer is no based on my willingness to hear Him and obey, but if I didn't it would get much worse and I'm sad to say, it did.

We dated for about 4 years and he decided he wanted a better job, so I paid for his CDL to help him. I was now working for the Houston Chronicle and in the daytime at a Home Health Agency, but I wanted a better job as well. I noticed he was different after getting a better job. He didn't have time for me. It was like I was a bother to him. I decided to take a Phlebotomy course at the local college to better myself. He became even more rude and insulting to me. I completed my course and had to do a three-week clinical rotation during the hours of 8am to 5pm which meant I would not be able to work at my daytime job where I got paid. He insulted me even more saying how stupid I was to quit a job that I made money on to do a clinical rotation where I didn't get paid. It took me 9 months to get a phlebotomy job after finishing that course, but God took care of all our needs. At the time I had my fifteen-year-old cousin living with me. It was tough, but God brought us through everything. When everyone else failed me, I learned to totally trust God. The only job I had was throwing papers making eight hundred dollars a month. Car note, rent, insurance, lights, food, gas, and our necessities were provided by God, because there is no way possible eight hundred dollars could have paid all that. God is a multiplier, when you believe.

I was finally able to get a phlebotomy job through a temporary service. All Praises to GOD and I was still throwing papers early morning. Things were looking up and I was feeling good for the moment. I wasn't communicating with him much, so I was good. I was leaving work after becoming a full-time employee of the actual company one evening when my cell phone rung and it was him. I could hear a lady screaming and yelling in the background. I finally asked who that was carrying on like that and he mumbled his wife. I said your who?!!! Your what?!!! At that point she must of, grabbed the phone because she started screaming in the phone asking how long I had been messing with her husband. She said they had two kids. I was totally speechless. It felt like a frog was sitting in my throat. However, I was not about to let her keep yelling at me because my world was just turned upside down as well. We briefly talked, and I found out they had been married a year. They got married the previous year on Valentine's Day and by this time we had been dating around 6 years. I can't believe that through it all I still had two children by this man. Our daughter was born in 2009 and our son in 2010, they are sixteen months apart.

Despite feeling enraged, I decided to entertain her. I told her that I saw him on Valentine's Day. He came to my apartment and left candy and bears on my bed saying he would be back later. Sad to say, her comment was, "oh that's where he went." Here I was again on this emotional roller coaster of pain, shame, guilt and embarrassment. I was so torn, and broken, it felt like my insides were bleeding. I deserved an explanation, I was the mother of this man's children or so I thought. So, I continued to talk to him. Sometimes I believe we lie or trick ourselves into believing I need an explanation when really, we need to just walk away. He gave me this story about how she forced him to marry her and he really loved me. Yes, I know all of this is a lie, but I wanted so desperately to believe him after all I'm in love, again! Shortly after this he got into trouble and went to prison and for three years I drove up and down the highway chasing him wherever the Texas Department of Criminal Justice sent him. I was convinced that I was doing all of this for love.

Let me reiterate this is the problem with us as women. When it's time to walk away and let go we don't, can't or won't. Now he's married to someone else and I owe him nothing, but because I didn't know my value or worth, I stayed. Let's be real this gave me a false sense of purpose. Yes, being used by someone who didn't want me made me think I was being purposeful. I didn't have a clue what my purpose was. It was all bottled up in me, but I wasn't doing myself any justice with these emotional decisions I was making.

Once he was released from prison, I gave him a car and money to help him get on his feet. This still wasn't good enough after all I had been through and done for this man. He left and went back to his wife, continuing to lie to me. He would run back and forward between the two of us, but I saw the signs and remembered all I had been through. I only got phone calls early in the morning around 5:00am to 6:00am when he's on his way to work. Then again about 5:30pm, right before going inside to his wife and kids. There were no other phone calls until the next morning. Ladies we have got to love ourselves more than this. We must learn how to let go and let God be our everything. We must learn to walk away and shake the dust off our feet. We must be willing to release ourselves from the emotional bondage that comes with men who have no clue how to be real men. Men with integrity and know how to honor, respect and treat a woman.

Even though I knew all of this I still couldn't walk away. I decided to move on and even though I didn't know how, I held on to the fact that God blessed me with two beautiful children out of the relationship. Only God can take a mess and create a masterpiece. Only God can create beauty out of ashes. I remember my daughter was 6 months old and I was pregnant again, with my son, they are 16 months apart. Someone started calling my home and cell phone, hanging up without saying a word, so I decided the next time this happens I was going to talk to this individual. Turns out it was a young lady who had just had a baby from him. This child was about two months old and she was born after my first daughter. At the point I was done. I told God that whenever He raised me up this guy will never have to worry about me ever again and I meant it.

Praise God I was free after eleven years of being used, abused and mistreated. I was finally able to let go. I still worked two jobs, bundling my babies up at night and throwing papers early in the morning. I worked at the blood lab in the daytime. My body was tired and a lot of days I didn't want to get up and go, but as a mother you will do what you must do to take care of your children. In November and December 2011, I experienced two major blows back to back. My sister died of cancer leaving four minor children behind and their father was in prison. Then my oldest brother passed two weeks after my sister. Leaving me no time to grieve and trying to dull the pain I found myself in another abusive relationship. In my opinion this one was the worst. He was a womanizer, liar, thief, user, and narcissistic. I became pregnant with my last child. I cried, cried, and cried some more! How was I possibly going to take care of another child, I was struggling to care for the first two.

I contacted the father and he seemed happy at first, but that quickly changed. He started saying he didn't believe me, and that I wasn't pregnant, so stop calling him. Again…crushed! I was on my own. I didn't want to be pregnant and thrown away like trash by a man like I never existed. I spent the entire pregnancy being hurt and angry, but God kept his hand over us and brought me through. The day came for my scheduled caesarean, which was January 25, 2013. I drove myself to the hospital and one of my brothers came to watch over my nieces and my other two children. I was alone and felt every bit of it. I finally called a cousin who lived an hour away and she drove down to Houston. I had my daughter and was battling in my mind to leave her at the hospital because I thought I was incapable of loving her. I thought she would be better off without me because my life was such a mess. I didn't tell my cousin what I was thinking or felt, but for the first twenty-four hours of my daughter's life I watched my cousin hold and love on her.

God will send you exactly what you need when you need it. She was there for my daughter to experience love because I was in no shape to love myself let alone her. I had been through so much in my life and so much had been taken, I felt I had nothing else left to give. My cousin asked repeatedly if I wanted to hold her and my answer was always no. I'm tired send her to the nursery. She badgered me all night long about holding my baby. I kept refusing. When the morning came, she said she had to leave and asked me one more time. I was so irritated with her, I just told her to give her to me. I bless God for that moment because that's all it took for me to hold her. She is one of the many joys of my life. I got out of the hospital and began to take care of those three precious gifts God gave to me. I was happy, life was good, God was good, I went back to church proudly with my three pieces.

You see God has a way of not allowing you to be ashamed of the mistakes you made. What he brought you out of and through is called a testimony. Life was good! I had been through a lot and survived it all, however, I was never delivered from all the abusive relationships. My heart was healed, but my mind was messed up. Failing to get to the root of my dysfunctional relationship choices and taking accountability for my brokenness caused me to travel down the same destructive path once again. I know I said this before, but he was truly the worst kind of abuser and I have suffered at the hands of a few.

Have you ever heard of a fruit roll-up? Well he was all …those guys I dated rolled up into one. The worst kind of abuser there is…he was charming, nice, inviting, thoughtful, understanding, caring, compassionate, loving, easy to talk to, a great listener, cooked, cleaned, worked and had his own business. He was just what the doctor ordered to fix any brokenness and hurting heart. If God was going to send a man who was the total package, he was truly the one. All these good traits were on the surface, but what lurked on the inside of him was much darker than anything I had ever seen, experienced or witnessed before. He had issues, and demons that ran deep within. Almost every day a different demon would introduce himself. He was a very hateful and disturbed individual.

Every woman desires to be loved and deserves true love, especially after all I'd been through in my lifetime. I can honestly say that I thought this was true love, but this was a very dangerous situation. It had become apparent that the enemy had it out for me and he was going to get me by any means necessary, especially using a man. Not only me, but also my children because it wasn't just me anymore. Whatever I experienced, they were going to experience the affects of it as well. In my mind he was a night in shining armor who came in and swept me off my feet. This was a lie from the pits of hell.

We worked at a warehouse together and I'd see him with his son and think to myself how sweet. Not long after that he initiated a conversation between us. Thinking back, it wasn't hard to see what I needed, here I am a single woman in the middle of the night delivering newspapers with my two small children. Both under the age of three and working a second job to make sure my kids and I didn't lack for anything. Then I was pregnant with a third child. Shortly after I had my third child, he began calling me. He would say things like, "Hey, baby this is your man Sam!"; or "Hey gorgeous how are you doing?"

I felt extremely flattered by these gestures making it very easy for me to be pulled into another bad relationship. Looking back, he was very aggressive towards me. He began to pop up, checking on me, bringing flowers and different gifts. He would take me out to dinner which is something I wasn't accustomed to after years of bad relationships. I was enjoying this extra attention. I felt extremely special and I hadn't really felt this in any other relationship. He continued to woo me with his cooking and not only me, but my children also. He always knew what to say, what to do and spent quality time with me and playing with my children. It wasn't long before we began spending quite a bit of time together. He seemed to really care about me or so I thought, and he made my life a little easier.

Eventually, he began talking about how much time we were spending between both households and suggested that we combine them into one. It did make sense and it sounded darn good, after all he was very caring and was good at pampering me, but that little inner voice was screaming...NOOOOO bad idea RUNNNN!

I was reluctant, but he turned up the charm even more and pushed me even harder in the direction he wanted me to go. I eventually gave in and looking back I now realize this is the point where I lost my voice. I stop thinking for myself and he had total control over me. He became the mastermind behind all my thoughts, pulling strings and making decisions without me knowing. He showed up with a moving truck while I was on maternity leave after giving birth to my daughter. He began to pack up all that I had hauling it off to a storage he rented which I had no idea where it was located (part of the controlling). I had an uncomfortable feeling about all of this but couldn't find my voice to speak up, so I didn't.

However, I reached out to my apartment manager telling her how fabulous my new boyfriend was and all the wonderful things he was doing. To be honest I was secretly looking for someone to stand up for me and stop me because I didn't have the courage to put a stop to all of this. Deep down inside I knew this wasn't right. My apartment manager told me that she would hold my apartment, just keep paying the rent just in case I needed to come back and I agreed. In March I paid the rent at my apartment, but in April I noticed that he was having issues paying the bills at his apartment. I told him that I was handling some personal bills and he told me to save my money and take care of my business. He asked if I was still paying rent at my apartment. I reluctantly said yes and instantly he became very upset with me, yelling about I only did that just in case things didn't work out with us. In my head, I was saying yes of course but he began to rant and rave for about an hour or more. So, for the month of April I snuck and paid my rent without him knowing. It appeared that things began to start calming down.

On April 20, 2013 early in the morning he snapped at me and began yelling and screaming as I was trying to get into bed because he said I scratched him. He stood up and got in my face telling me to get out as I stood there crying saying "what" not understanding. He grabs his son, wraps him in a blanket and says since you won't leave then I will. It was three o'clock in the morning. My apartment was totally empty, and I had nothing there. I was too embarrassed at this point to go back. My baby was three months old and it was very cold outside, so I stayed. The next morning, I was still feeling confused and reconsidering my decision. I was not liking the way I was being treated and talked too. Out of the blue he calls me on my cell phone. Saying did something happen last night? I said yes you were very rude to me yelling and screaming and I don't appreciate it. He just blew me off by saying well I don't remember any of that and I'm busy at work, so I don't have time to talk about this with you (mind control).

At that moment, it left me feeling so empty inside knowing what a horrible mistake I had made not sure how to get out of it. As the day's progressed, he pumped up the charm once again. I came home to a cooked dinner, the kids bath water had been ran and my lunch was already packed for the next day. Wow, I thought to myself this is nice, maybe it's not so bad after all. Maybe it's ME! Maybe it's my behavior; something I said or did. The next morning I'd get up for work and my son would be dressed, my baby would be ready while I dressed my oldest daughter. He would go downstairs and get my vehicle ready. All I had to do was walk down stairs, where my coffee would be poured and head out the door. I really enjoyed being waited on hand and foot, but by the weekend he'd be a totally different person. The constant yelling, threating to throw me and my kids out on the street, belittling me and saying how I was nobody and not even worthy of being married would start all over again. I can remember him laughing at me saying you so stupid all you have is a high school diploma. I have college degrees and served in the marine corps. What have you done for the country? I simply replied well my high school education seems to be paying these bills you can't afford, so how is those college degrees working for you now? He had a cut on his right hand, and I asked him how did he get it? That seemed to make him angry and he starting yelling saying he wasn't allowed to talk about it. It happened to him when he was serving our country. An enemy caught him sleeping and killed his buddy and when he woke up, there was a man attempting to cut his hand off. I'm not making any excuses for him whatsoever, but whatever he experienced in the military or just in life period, caused him to be a very vile person.

Ladies it is very hard to hold yourself up emotionally and keep going after being beat down to the lowest of the low on a daily base. As much as you hope for change, without God it is literally impossible. He became more and more angrier and fowl with each passing day. I spent most of the days trying to be invisible, yet perfect. There is nothing like peace and freedom. We must love ourselves enough to know our value and our worth. We can't continue to settle for anything less than Gods best. Even though many of us were not taught our value as children or it was stolen from us by people who were monsters, we still have a responsibility to look in the mirror and find it for ourselves. You must understand that not all discounts are bargains.

Chapter Four

"Losing Myself to A Narcissist"

As time went on the outburst, verbal, mental and emotional abuse grew worse and I still had no idea what I was dealing with. I called my old apartment complex to ask the manager who was my friend, if she still had my apartment because what was going on with him didn't seem or feel right. My lease was up at the end of May; therefore, the apartment had already been leased to someone else. Feeling sick to my stomach and stuck I didn't know what else to do. He began to be threating towards my three-year-old daughter saying how he would throw her over the balcony. He would stand over her and call her inappropriate names like the 'B' word, yes, a female dog. She was a three-year-old child who posed no threat to him at all. I was fearing for my children and ashamed of the poor decision I made not knowing where to turn. I kept my children close to me. I took them wherever

I went and often called on my good friend Bertha to take my baby allowing her to stay with her weeks at a time. This was my way of protecting her. I would call on my siblings to keep the two oldest children. I never explained what was going on, I just wanted to get them away from the tension, even if for the weekend. I would even stay in motel rooms with my children just to get away and get some sleep without looking over my shoulder or watching my back. I did this often, so I'd know my children were safe, but nothing last forever. My children and I could not keep going like this during the week so I would come back to the apartment. He shows up one day out of nowhere with a ring telling me how he was going to surprise me, but he thought he'd just go ahead and give it to me.

These types of guys are very attentive and plan everything. This was just a trick to keep me around a little longer because he knew by my behavior, I was looking for a way out. He also began to tell me we should open a bank account and put both our names on it. Well come to find out the ring belonged to his wife who had run away from him. The bank account was another way to control me through my finances. According to him this would be the account we use to pay bills and both our checks would go into this account. This was a lie. I told him okay, well it required that we both go to start the account. He insisted I go without him, however, I insisted he go as well. So, we went together to my Credit Union I was banking with at that time. After sitting down and giving our information they ran checks on both of our names and came back with a no for him which I now know he knew all along just trying to fool me and leave me holding any consequences, but I was in love so I couldn't see pass it. He began to explain how his ex-wife wrote some bad checks on him. I began thinking to myself this isn't making sense and it just sounded like a pack of lies.

This made me look at him in an even worse way, because I now know the mind games he was playing. As days went by, I saw more and more narcissistic behavior. One day I was looking on his desk that sat in the living room which we were not allowed to touch, and things were just off about this whole situation. As I listened to the many stories about his life, I found out later they were all lies, or someone else's story he made his own. This is classic for abusive, narcissistic men. I found a book of checks with my name and his name, my routing and bank account number to my Chase account. This didn't make any sense because we didn't have an account together, so where did these checks come from? I asked myself this rhetorical question, because I already knew he wasn't going to be honest. I dropped it for the moment and didn't say a word fearing being put out on the streets with my babies. Things became more uncomfortable for me and my children.

I couldn't touch his food, or he would lock me outside pretending to be asleep and accidently lock the top lock. He would slide the big screen TV to the middle of the floor and turn the volume up to the max to keep me awake in order to keep me off balance. His ways were beyond ugly, and we needed out. I can remember getting off work early one day and I went to the apartment hoping to relax as much as I could. His cell phone rings and he had a very strange look on his face while looking at me. He reaches his hand out handing me his cell phone saying it's for you. I get on the phone and he was sitting very close looking directly at me as if to hear what is being said on the other end. It was, one of the bankers from Chase bank who informed me that there was unusual activity occurring with my bank account. These were transactions not within my normal banking spending habits. Therefore, he was reaching out to see what was going on?

I personally had no idea about what he was speaking of because I hadn't done much at all. As a matter of fact, I was saving as much as I possibly could. I had been planning to get out of there one day soon at least that's what my mind was thinking, but my heart was disagreeing. As I sat quietly grasping everything he's saying and thinking why he would be calling his phone instead of mine, he's not on my account. How did he even get his number to call him? I stayed calm and said okay thank you for calling, but in my mind, I needed answers. As soon as I hung up, he asked what was all that about, I replied they were just checking on my account because its new, seeing if there is anything, they could help me with. I lied!

The very next day I made my way into the bank to see exactly what was going on. I met with the same guy who I had spoken with on the phone the day before. As we talked, he informed me that my bank card had been used at several different ATM machines around the local area and online. We began to look up the transactions and withdrawals which had occurred during the hours I was at work. There was a purchase for checks which I questioned because I get my checks directly from Chase and I never order them online. As we talked about that I informed the banker about the checks I found on his desk. He explained to me about the websites online that design checks to say exactly what you want them to say. Now I knew where the checks came from. He also explained there had been a lot of changes to my account including all my contact information. Which also explained why he called his cell phone and not mine. The more we talked, we arrived at closing the account and canceling the ATM card. I had to reset and change all my information assigning special passwords and additional security measures to insure this would not happen again.

I told the banker I didn't want an ATM card and had no clue as to where to put my new banking information. My vehicle and his apartment were not safe, so I decided to find a hiding place at my job. I didn't say a word to him about any of this when I returned. However, that night I decided it was time to leave. I didn't know where we were going, but I needed out. He said he had to work early that morning and he came home around 2:00am in the morning intoxicated. So, I waited and planned my escape as he was still sleeping. I began to pack up the few items we had there but once he walked out into the living room realizing there were somethings missing, he quickly turned things around. Suddenly he wasn't going into work. He asked what was going on and I told him I wanted to leave. My baby was laying in her bed. My two older children were up as he made a dash to the front door, and so did I; following him not sure where he was going or what he would do. He immediately ran down stairs and start letting the air out of the tires to my SUV. I asked what was, he doing? And please stop, my baby was upstairs sleeping, and my two older children had come down the stairs following me as I stood there pleading with him not to let the air out. Just let us leave! Immediately after letting the air out of the tire he pulled his cell phone out called a tow truck saying it was an abandoned vehicle in the parking lot. He called out my license plate number and a description of my vehicle. I was very upset and crying, as we were walking upstairs, he turns around to me saying now you must get out of my apartment you are trespassing.

He pulls out his cell phone again. Making another call he begins to say, "Yes I need your help I need you to do something for me can you come over here I'll explain it to you." I say to him who did you call? Smiling at me with this awkward devious smile he said, "Oh don't you worry about that you will see I'm going to have your butt thrown in jail to teach you a lesson and Detective Morris would lose you in the system for a few days." I started crying even more asking what about my children? He smiles at me and says they will be just fine, but you need to spend some time in jail. Detective Morris (whom he had threatened me with before saying he was one of his police officer buddies) is coming over to lock you up in jail to teach you a lesson. He goes inside shutting the door in my face. He comes back and hands me my baby through the door then locks it, leaving us outside on the steps. I sat outside on the stairs with my three babies crying, no cell phone to call anyone, stressed, tired and hadn't had a decent night's sleep in a while. I couldn't help but worry about my babies. How I failed them as a mother waiting on whatever or whoever was to come, because at this point, I was broken and didn't feel as if I had any fight left in me. Hours later he pops open the front door like he was just opening his fine restaurant for the day, inviting diners in to dine, like the last few hours never happened. Saying, come on in why are you sitting out here? I stared at him in disbelief after all the chaos that had just took place.

I looked at my babies who were hot, tired and hungry and looking at me through their innocent eyes feeling bad, so I went back inside. He begins to tell me what he was going to cook for the day and how much he loved me and didn't want me to leave, as if nothing never happened. I stayed, feeling trapped, too shame to use my voice to let anyone know what I was going through. After all I told everyone how great of a man he was. How could I go back and tell people what was really going on? Feeling like I needed him to survive, not wanting to go to jail. Things were good for a week then suddenly he was back at it again, yelling screaming and hollering. I had to come up with a plan, so I thought some things through. I came up with leaving one of my vehicles at my night time job where he had been banned from the premises for fighting with one of the young men who worked there.

I got one of my coworkers to give me a ride to the apartment, so I could slip away a little easier. I had this all figured out. I would wait for him to leave and grab a few things and just go. It didn't matter where, I just needed out for my own sanctity. I felt like I was losing my mind. It was spinning in a downward spiral. However, he must have sensed me getting ready to make a move because he stayed home all day frequently going from inside to outside. He noticed my Chevrolet Equinox was missing so he began to question me about it. My reluctant answers angered him. He begins yelling at me about me not being a good person, a liar, being sneaky, and hateful which was extremely funny because he had just described himself in detail to me. I didn't get to leave this day, but I began to study him and my situation because something had to give. June 1, it was rent time, but I had started putting money aside secretly from my own check, so I didn't have any extra money just what I needed to take care of me and my little ones. He informed me he did not have money to pay rent. I told him neither did I. His comment to me was well I guess we will be out on the streets. I didn't entertain him any farther so as the next couple days passed, I didn't hear anything else about the rent money. Friday morning, I was running late to get to work on time and I left my cell phone by accident at the apartment, however, I did have a phone in my SUV. I dropped my kids at daycare and headed to the blood laboratory in Friendswood a great company I had worked at since 2003. The phone in the truck started ringing and it was him saying why didn't you tell me the rent check bounced? My response was, "I didn't know anything about that since I didn't write a check for this month rent."

He begins to yell at me saying, the office staff is at the door saying that are about to lock him and his son outside the door. Then he hangs the phone up in my face. Automatically I'm upset, and I call him back he picks up yelling, hanging up again in my face, I try once more he does the same thing now, I've arrived at work. Clearly, I'm upset I go into work because I don't understand any of this at all and that's not how an eviction work, and where did the check come from, I discover I don't have my cell phone, so I used the landline at work calling him back. I say to him I don't know anything about what's going on, but we still must solve the issue at hand because it seems the rent had not been paid, again he hangs the phone up in my face. It's now 7:30am and the doors to the lab are now open. My coworker is ready to receive patients and I can't focus. The phone rings at the lab. I answer and its him yelling at me about not speaking to him the way I had just done, he always had to be in control. I say to him I must go I'm at work please don't call here with that as I gather myself, so I can start servicing patients. He continues to call. I told my coworker somewhat of what was going on and not to answer the phone.

Somehow, I manage to get through half of the day with all of this on my mind. It's now 12:00pm lunchtime and I go to lunch first, heading to the apartment to grab my cell phone I quickly run in grabbing my cell phone on my way out the door I noticed he has left his black zipper conference folder on the counter which never happens. I decide to quickly look opened it and the first thing I saw was a copy of my birth certificate, my three children's as well, and a copy of all four of our social security cards and a copy of my driver license. I took all those copies out closing the folder and hurrying back to work taking the copies with me, this is very odd and not making sense to me why would he have copies of our personal information. I finish my day at work once I clocked out. I sat in my truck trying to gather my thoughts and not wanting to go back to the apartment because I just don't want to deal with this mess. I'm extremely tired! Slowly I made my way to pick my children up from daycare. I found myself sitting in the daycare parking lot after getting my children dreading going to that apartment. Slowly, I made my way there only to find myself sitting in the parking lot of the apartments.

Finally, I got out with my kids walking slowly upstairs as soon as I walked in, he says to me this is over I'm shutting this down I went to the office and bought out of my lease as of Monday we all must be out. Looking back my perfect response would have been how is that possible when you can't even pay the rent for the month let alone buyout the remainder of your lease, however I wasn't thinking. He then begins to remind me of how he was helping me and my children but now that is over. Well, he was just getting started with the normal confusing, I was tired I told him ok that's fine but I'm not going to wait until Monday my kids and I would leave tonight. I called my oldest two kid's father asking if he could help me move. I explained we could no longer live there, and I needed his help moving and driving my vehicles. He told me he would come help but make sure I was going to leave I said yes of course I would leave, this was the first time I had told anyone about anything that I was going through. As I waited, I noticed my cell phone battery was dying so I went to the kitchen plugged it up to a charger sat back down in a chair with my kids sitting at my feet.

After a little while I told my kids to sit there and not move, I was going to look to see if I could see their dad at the gate trying to get in because I would have to let him through the gate. I didn't see him, so I went back inside going to pick up my phone to see if he had called me. However, my phone was gone I looked around the counter top and floor no phone. I asked him had he taken my phone? His response you didn't pay for it, it's not your phone I said hey you asked me to leave I'm trying to do that. I had it charging now please give it back, his response you didn't pay for the charger, my patience was running thin with him, so I walked over to him and said give it back. He threw the phone at me. I didn't care that he threw it at me. I picked it up and I immediately called their father to see where he was. He said close I'm almost there and Carolyn I'm not by myself I brought three of my friends with me. At that moment I didn't care who he had bought I was just ready to leave. I waited a little while longer and I went outside looking and seen him following another vehicle through the gate. I waited for him on the top of the stairs as they made their way upstairs. We all walked to the apartment, I knocked on the door saying hey, can they come in referring to the guys that came to help me. He replies, sure yes of course so politely like why wouldn't they? At this point I am realizing he lie and play so many games he thought no one was coming to help me.

Like I was bluffing the whole time about leaving. I began to point to the things I was taking like my baby bed, kids toddler beds, stroller, kid's clothes, some of my clothes, things are moving alone as he sits on the couch quietly. My kids father comes back up and says "Man this is ridiculous, and I don't appreciate what you said to my daughter. He my abuser jumps up off the couch saying you don't know what you are talking about by this time the three young men had made it back upstairs. Curtis tells Sam don't you ever threaten my daughter. Sam tells Curtis that's hear say you didn't hear me say that. Sam puts his hand under his shirt in the back of his pants as if he had a gun walking up to Curtis slowly. Curtis says let's go we can do this. I immediately jump in the middle between them saying wait, wait, wait. Sam walks backwards as if not to let us see what's behind his back. He comes back to the door with his cell phone saying, "Yes, we need the police over here we got guns out getting ready to blaze and go at it."

I stood there speechless because he was lying, and I could hear one of the young men behind me saying you lying nobody has guns out. Sam continues, on the phone and says Carolyn you must step out until the police get here. I step out and he locks the door. I turn to Curtis, upset saying why didn't you just be quiet a little longer I was almost done getting my things out of there. I told Curtis as we were waiting for the police to show up, to leave if he had warrants are anything he would get in trouble for. Curtis told me he was fine he wasn't going anywhere. I told Curtis my tags on my Equinox were expired and we should move that vehicle off the premises because Sam would try to get me in trouble or whoever drove it off the property in trouble. Curtis said it would be fine just wait for the officers to show. We waited about thirty minutes and I told Curtis this is taking a while, so I will call back to see what's going on as we all waited downstairs in the parking lot. I called the non-emergency line for Houston police Department and I gave the operator the address and he asked me was I at Mr. Gill address. I said yes, the operator explained they had called back and spoke with Sam because it was a dial and hang up that came from his phone. When they called back Sam told them everything was fine. In fact, he said his son was playing with his phone and he apologized for the hang up assuring them everything was fine at his address and nothing more.

I instantly became upset and said none of that is true and we do need an officer to come out. I explained to the operator what had taken place up to that point. I was informed an officer was being dispatched to our location as we spoke. Once hanging up I told Curtis what the operator informed me of. I began to think if he was speaking to the police earlier about guns blazing, they would have swarmed in that place so fast. They would have put all of us on the ground in handcuffs including kids and all until they could sort through what was going on. This was just another sad attempt at controlling the situation and keeping me there. I got in my truck with my children. I called T-Mobile, attempting to port my cell number over to an extra phone I kept because I knew how devious Sam could be. The officer arrived before I could finish getting my phone number ported over. She instructed me to get out and hang up the phone, so she could speak with me.

I explained to her I only wanted to finish getting my things so I could leave. She asked did he have guns and I told her I never seen any, but he often would refer to his guns. She told me she would have to call for backup for her safety, so just sit tight. We did as the officer asked, but while waiting, Sam came walking down the stairs. You can just imagine the look on his face once he saw the officer. She asked him to come over and he replied, I don't have to talk to you. She said, "Yes, but we are trying to settle this matter." He still refused and by this time a second police cruiser arrived with two additional officers. There was an older white gentleman, and a young Hispanic guy. All three of the officers gathered together to discuss the matter. Sam headed back upstairs. The older officer told me there was nothing they could do because this was a civil matter. He said I would have to go to my local justice of the peace and file to get my belongings.

I told the officer I needed to get my uniforms for work, like the one I had on with my company name on it and he said I couldn't. The only way they would intervene if there was medicine that was needed. I told him my children's medications and breathing machines were in the first cabinet to the left in the kitchen. The officer headed upstairs to get them for me. He returned empty handed saying Sam told him I took all of that. I broke down and started crying because that was a lie, he was never going to just let me walk away, he was an evil person. My children have bronchitis and asthma that require those machines and medications. How could anyone purposely withhold medicine and treatment from innocent children or anyone for that matter? The officers were instructing us to vacate the premises. Sam comes running down the stairs saying her tags are expired on that truck over there, referring to my Equinox.

I turned to look at Curtis with that I told you so look on my face. The officers didn't say anything but again instructed us to leave. Sam then says to the officers "Hey are you going to just let her leave with both of the vehicles?" The older officer replied, "Whose name are the vehicles in?" I said the Equinox is in just my name, but the Tahoe is in both our names. Sam begins yelling you can't just let her leave me without a car. The female officer who was first on the scene said, "Sir this is the first time you said anything about a vehicle the whole time it's been about property." By this time everyone's patience seemed to be wearing with Sam because he was wasting everyone's time. The officers said to Sam she's trying to leave like you asked so just let her. I got into the Tahoe with my two older children, so we could leave. Sam became angry that this wasn't going his way and jumped in the back seat of the Tahoe saying wherever she's going with this truck so am I.

The officers begin to tell him to get out of the vehicle he can't do that. Sam refused to get out, Curtis came over and got into the front seat, Sam quickly jumped out of the back seat. The officers had me blocked in. One said let me move the cruiser and as soon as I do you guys get out of here, and so we did. We all drove off regrouping at the Food Town store at the corner away from the apartments. Curtis who is a truck driver told me he had to go out of town that night to work. As he and I were talking, I decided to check my cell phone and just as I knew he would Sam had it turned off. Curtis told me he would park the Equinox at a relative house.

We decided to move a little farther down the road away from that area. As we are driving, I hear my phone make a noise. I pulled over again into a parking lot and checked my phone. Sam had the phone turned back on and sent a text message saying, "You have twenty-four hours with your phone, so you better take care all your business within that time. I will be mailing your items you left to your sister house." I'm sitting in my vehicle crying thinking he couldn't even pay his rent how is he going to mail anything? I found a motel room to stay for the night. Sam began to call and text about how he loved me, how sorry he was, and how we needed to fix this. He even started trying to cry on the phone. I fell for it and was back the next morning at the apartment. What was I thinking? Lord help me but when you are trapped in your mind you will believe or do anything.

Chapter Five

"Painfully Fragmented"

Brokenness – having been fractured or damaged and no longer in one piece or in working order; (of a person) having given up all hope; despairing.

The above definition described every facet of my being during that season of my life. I wasn't broken just because of Sam; my brokenness began with the first violation as a little girl. The problem was Carolyn was trying to play God and put the broken pieces back together and as you can see, I was only making it worse. I was taking the few pieces I had left and allowing them to be grinded down to nothing. Literally non-existent. I was no longer living in a realistic world, with hopes and dreams. I was living in a nightmare that I didn't have the power to wake up and stay WOKE. I would wake up for a little while and then fall right back into the nightmare. Ladies, please be mindful that this is NOT the will of God for His precious Daughters. We were fearfully and wonderfully made by God.

I went back, but things were still spiraling out of control. I was in jeopardy of losing everything. As if I hadn't lost enough already. My storage unit was about to be auctioned off, if I didn't come up with the money. Sam finally decided to tell me that the bill hadn't been paid for months. He suggested finding a smaller more affordable unit to store my belongings. This was a wonderful idea because this meant my storage would no longer be close to the office location that he rented. I found another storage location and put my name on the contract. I can recall an incident that occurred after I got of work. I had been up most of the morning rolling news papers for work and was extremely exhausted. When I got home, Sam approached me about moving the stuff in storage into the new unit. I suggested another time, but he insisted, so I went. We were able to load the stuff on the truck and keep in mind, it was just me and him. Well, when we arrived at the new storage, he was standing on the back of the truck, throwing the boxes down at me. As he threw the boxes, he would laugh, because I kept falling. This was the most insensitive thing ever and I was sick of it.

Slowly I would take small amounts of our clothes out of his apartment; little by little, taking it to the new storage facility. I informed Curtis to hold the items we had removed from Sam's apartment in June. I began to look around for a place to live. I spent all of July prepping myself to leave, searching for apartments and putting things into storage for my kids and myself without saying a word to Sam. Towards the end of July Sam comes to me with this off the wall idea.

He wanted to get custody of his son and someone told him he could go live in a shelter for thirty days. During his stay they would help him pay rent, get a fresh start, and have access to legal services. I later found out that he was really going into the shelter to hide because he was wanted for embezzling money from a carpet cleaning business that he owned. One day he came and said he was going to the Star of Hope located in Downtown, Houston to try this. Well, I thought to myself, good, especially if that meant him not being there with us. I didn't know if he was bluffing, but in August he left, and I was loving it. I finally had peace of mind and no Sam. I could have thrown a party I was so happy. He would pop in and out telling me how he was progressing at the shelter. He would talk about all the things that the shelter was doing and going to do for him. Nothing but a bunch of lies. As usual he was up to something. He was talking about them finding him an apartment, paying his rent for six months, and helping him with utilities. He said he found an apartment close to where his son could go to school. Since he served in the military it would be paid for. More lies I might add.

This started me to thinking, why would he need another apartment? What about the one he currently had? It was at that point a light bulb went off in my head. I realized he couldn't afford the apartment, so his plan was to leave me there to finish paying the duration of his lease. It made me think of all the other things he had said so I looked for Steve's number, Sam's brother. I needed some answers. I normally kept my distance, because of the many horrible things Sam told me about him. I was at work one day and I called Steve, he was very polite. I said hey I know you might not want to answer any of my questions, and I understand but I'm trying to figure out what is going on with your brother. I told him Sam had left saying he was going into a shelter leaving me there at the apartment. Steve said, "Sam told us he no longer has that apartment." Imagine my shock! I said well that's not true because my kids and I are still here. Steve informed me Sam told them I had took off with my kids. He asked if the kids and I, could stop by their townhome that night to come and talk with him and his wife. I said ok feeling a little uneasy, however that night I didn't go by there, but I did call. Steve put the phone on speaker, so I was able to speak with them at the same time. I told Steve, how Sam described him, his own brother as a very jealous person, who had slept with his old girlfriend and how Steve used Sam for money.

I mentioned Sam being in the marines for twenty years and retired. Suddenly I heard a burst of laughter on the line from Steve and his wife. Steve asked me to hold on he wanted to call his sister and get her on the line. I said of course. Steve introduced me as Sam's girlfriend and the sister was shocked because Sam had contacted her in February saying he would be going to jail for a while. So, he wouldn't be able to talk with her. I said wow that's when I got here. The sister says to me Carolyn pack your stuff and get you and your kids far away from there. My brother is not a good person and he will drag you down. Steve says Carolyn tell her about Sam and the military. Then the sister bust out laughing saying that's a lie. Sam never graduated from high school, however my husband is twenty years marine.

At that point Steve says to me Carolyn anything he has told you turn it around. He's talking about himself. He's a liar. At this point I'm floored, and realize I'm dealing with a psychopath. I must get out no matter how I feel, or what my heart says, because this situation is not safe for anyone. According to Steve, the cut on his hand was not military related. It was from a lady who he stole money from. 1st Corinthian 15:33 says, "Don't be misled, bad company corrupts good character." This bad company was draining me and the whole time making me look like a fool. When he was the one with the problem. He was the one with the insecurities. He was just as broken and jacked up as he was making me. He was determined to make my life as miserable as by any means necessary.

On August 31st, Sam has the unmitigated gall to call me and ask me to pay his rent. I decided it was time to take a stand once and for all. I told him no. Then he told me that I had to go and be out of his apartment by the time he got there. Franticly, I started calling and reaching out to people because this was my chance to get out. First, I needed to find shelter for us. I called a good friend who I refer to as my brother, Ron, explaining truthfully what was going on with me and what had transpired over the last 6 months. He asked me why I hadn't said anything because we shouldn't be going through that. In fact, he had moved in with his girlfriend, therefor, my kids and I could go to his apartment. I was scared so I began to look around. There was a file cabinet kept in his bedroom as I looked in it, I found different medical bills from what appeared to be women who had previously lived there.

Sam called threating me once again about what he would do to me. I was scared so I called the police once again. Two officers came I told them what was going on and they said you need to get somewhere safe and protect your children. The officers looked at each other without saying anything then one asked me was the guy from Opelousas, Louisiana. I said yes and at that moment I realized this wasn't the first time he had did something like this and they knew exactly who he was. I gave my information and Sam's also. The officers went outside and when they came back, they offered me information about shelters and another case report number. I took the information and they told me to get somewhere safe and they would be on duty for the night, and if he came to call 911. They said they would be in the area. I reached out to another good friend by the name of Wendell. I explained what was going on and he told me he would be right over. Ron came over to give me the keys to his apartment. My emotions were all over the place, but the top one was fear. I called Wendell who is a young man I became friends with at the warehouse. I met Wendell when he came to work for the Houston Chronicle, he was 27 years old at that time. I would roll my papers outside, because I had my two older children with me and wanted them to be as comfortable as possible considering the circumstances. Wendell and I became friends and would roll our papers outside together talking away about anything that came to mind. Our friendship grew and we became closer as the years went by. So, once Wendell found out about the domestic violence, I was enduring he wanted to help. However, I didn't want to change my situation at that time. I wasn't ready to let go.

Wendell was very patient and understanding even though he didn't agree with my way of dealing with my current situation. Which really wasn't dealing with it at all. I can recall several times after Wendell finding out how I was being treated he came to our rescue. I can remember him calling one day in June saying hey you alright over there. I said no I have no money and my kids are hungry. He was upset over the phone. I could tell not at me but the situation. He abruptly said I will call you back. He called me back in about thirty minutes saying hey, can you come outside, or do you want me to come upstairs. I said oh no I'll come to you. Sam had gone into his room hours prior, locking the door with us having no access to the restroom. Plus, I didn't want to cause any trouble for Wendell. He purchased some hot food for me and my kids from a restaurant. Not only was I not allowed in the kitchen, but I wasn't allowed to touch his food. So, Wendell bought some extra groceries just for us.

I remember a time in July when Wendell called and said, "Hey beautiful!" To be honest I was feeling anything, but beautiful. He said, "Can you and the kids meet me, or do you want me to pick you up?" I didn't want to be responsible for causing any confusion, so I decided to meet him. He said, great I will be waiting at the corner. I gathered my three kids and met up with him. He told me to follow him. We drove to a restaurant on Bay Area Blvd called Ichibon. It was a buffet and we was hungry. So, we were very excited. I had a sudden rush of emotions, where I wanted to cry, because he had no idea that we hadn't been eating. At least I hadn't told him. Sam would cook before we arrived at the apartment. We could still smell the aroma of food in the air, but there wouldn't be any food in site. Everything would be gone, and the kitchen would be spotless. Then he would lock himself up in the room, cutting off access to the only restroom in the apartment. Wendell showing up for me and my kids taught me that God will do for us, the things we can't do for ourselves. He is a faithful and just God that looks past our faults and sees our needs. Yes, my situation was jacked up and one that I put myself in, and even though I was condemning myself, God wasn't condemning me. He was waiting for me to choose "Him" and then myself. I was getting close, but I hadn't fully gotten there just yet.

Wendell and I never talked about this, but if he's reading this he now knows and should know how much I thank him for looking out for me and my kids when I couldn't. I called Wendell telling him what was going on with me and the kids, he told me to sit tight he was on his way. I said here meaning to Sam's apartment, he said yes. I was thinking of the mess before with Curtis and didn't want to be responsible for anyone getting in trouble or even hurt trying to help me. Wendell told me he was a big boy and could handle himself, not to worry. Wendell showed up about 11:00pm that night. We talked briefly about what transpired. Wendell started moving the few items I had. It wasn't much at all. A few baskets of clothes, pictures here and there, a small number of dishes and towels. I left the key on the counter, walked down the stairs to leave and told Wendell to get out of there. He looked at me saying, Carolyn I'm a big boy I can handle myself you go get out of here. I got into my Tahoe with my three children. Wendell tapped on the back window as to say, you are clear go.

You are clear to go! That sounded like music to my ears. All this time I was trying to figure out how to get away. The nights I stayed up crying and contemplating, but nothing seemed to work out right. But now I was in my car, with my kids, about to leave this demonic hell hole I had dug for myself and my babies. I put the truck in drive and suddenly this sense of freedom and release came over me. I can only imagine how the woman felt when Jesus told her, "Woman thou art loosed!" As I was driving there were a wealth of emotions that I was dealing with, but the most important was knowing that my babies were now safe. I didn't really care about me at this point. I made a choice that directly affected them and now I had to step into mommy recovery mode.

We arrived at the apartment in Friendswood. We went inside to get settled and that night I slept like I hadn't in almost seven months. I woke up refreshed and rejuvenated. I was ready to tackle the world. I didn't realize how drained and emotionally distraught I really was. My cell phone started to go off and it was a text message from Sam asking if I was out of his apartment. I ignored the message. The next text message was from AT&T saying you are being located and it had Sam's cell number on it. I got scared and turned the phone off. I turned it back on several hours later to discover, he had my phone disconnected. This wasn't a big surprise because he was petty like that. That made me mad. I reached into my belongings and found my T-Mobile phone. I called to have the phone activated. I blocked my number and called his phone to leave a message that he hadn't done anything because I still had my phone. The joke was on him, or so I thought. Soon the joke again would be on me.

Chapter Six

"From Bad to Worse – The Stalker"

September 2nd was a Monday. I was enjoying my newfound freedom. I drove to my beautician to get my hair done. I had a court date on the third of September. I enjoyed the rest of my day on the second and got up on the third of September, dropped my children off at daycare and headed to downtown Houston for child support court. Court went great. I headed back to pick my kids up from daycare, but I stopped at the grocery store first. Then I went to the bank and picked up some Popeyes chicken. We arrived at the apartment and I took the kids inside and fixed their food. I headed back outside to get the groceries when my truck says find me. There was no broken glass, therefore, I knew that Sam was behind this. I can't even begin to explain how I felt at that moment. I just wanted to be left alone. I just wanted the opportunity to have some peace, take care of my kids and move forward with my life. I always heard people say, "Don't mess with the devil, if you don't want to get burned." Well, I heard it, but now I was living it. That demon was coming for me by any means necessary and he wasn't letting up. With all the millions of other women in the world that he could torment, he chose to keep coming for me. Which paints an even clearer picture that we wrestle not against flesh and blood. Sam was on assignment from the enemy to destroy my life and I was not about to give up without a fight. Was I tired? Of course! But I had three innocent children looking at me for guidance, protection, and love. Even if I didn't do it for myself, I had to fight for them.

The first thing I did was block my number and call him. I started screaming for him to bring my truck back. He started laughing and said I would never see my truck again. He said it was on the way to Louisiana. He so called arranged for his people to come and get it. I hung up and called the police. This time it was two sheriffs who showed up and when I explained what was going on, they did the usual. They gave me an incident number, told me to get a restraining order and find a shelter for protection. I couldn't for the life of me understand how this man could keep getting away with this foolishness, while me and my babies had to keep being inconvenienced. This mess is exhausting, and I know this doesn't make any sense, but sometimes you go back just because you don't have the energy to keep wrestling over nothing. You can't get any proper help from those who are supposed to protect and serve, so it leaves you feeling vulnerable, hopeless and helpless.

The next day was September 4th and Sam began sending me messages through Facebook Messenger with several disturbing threats. He wanted to make a deal to get my truck back. He threatened to get me fired from my job. Then this crazy dude would ask how the baby is doing? The constant mind games had become overwhelming and I was sick and tired of being sick and tired. He would go from nice to mean with the snap of a finger. I got a call from a detective at the Friendswood Police Department who said he was looking for me. He had gotten a call from Chase Bank because someone there had placed a call expressing concern for me. My mind was baffled. I didn't believe it was a detective. I even told him that I didn't believe him, because Sam had played so many games. Not to mention I had got that cell number days before so none of this was making sense. How would this detective have my number? The detective assured me he was who he said he was. He gave me a number to call back to the station, but I still didn't believe him. I did call back and spoke with the detective at the number provided by him. He informed me he was coming to get me. Once he got there, he would knock a certain way and I would know it was him. I waited and about ten minutes later there was a very loud knock on the door. I tipped to the door peeking through the peak hole. It was the detective who had come to help me.

This is where my life officially changed. On Wednesday September 4, 2013, my children and I were taken to Bay Area Turning Point. The detective came to get us with a liaison and two uniform officers. I was strongly encouraged by all that showed up to assist. They kept telling me that I needed to be somewhere safe and my response was I thought I was safe. I was then told I needed to be thinking about my children and do the right thing as I looked upon their small faces at ages, four, three, and eight months old. I agreed to go to a shelter as the liaison made the call looking for shelter for us. I could hear her speaking to the person on the line saying but she has nowhere to go and has three small children. So, you will have to make room. At that moment, it hit me - we were homeless with nowhere to go. We had no place to live while being haunted like wild animals. All these years of chasing men, looking for love, giving all that I had, enduring abuse, to have nothing to show for it. I had been bankrupted in every area of my life. The only thing I had was my life and the lives of my children and I had to suck it up and realize that was enough to press for another hour, because at this point, I didn't know what each day would bring. I had already taken enough leaps. It was time to take some baby steps. It was time for Carolyn to get out of the way and allow God to get in the way. Fully in the way!

I sucked up whatever tears were forming, put a smile on my face and smiled through my tears, so my children wouldn't catch on to how bad things really were and were about to get. I was told to quickly gather a few items of clothing for myself and the children. We were put into an SUV with the liaison. The detective followed behind us in an unmarked car. The two uniform officers both in their own patrol cars split up setting up at different points as they looked out for any sign of my abuser. Once arriving at the office of Bay Area we were escorted into the building and put into a room awaiting intake. I started looking around the room and immediately broke down crying. I could no longer hold my tears back because it was all real at that moment. This was my life I was looking at and it had been altered at the snap of a finger. My two older children came over and began wiping my tears and hugging me. A lady came in introducing herself and asking me to follow her to an office to complete intake information. They needed to assess our needs for protection. The information I had to give was very detailed and personal.

She asked if I had a cell phone and to let her see it. I told her I had two, but he had the one connected with his service turned off. So, I turned the power off. She told me I had to take the battery out because even though it had no service it could still be tracked. After naming my abuser and giving all the needed information I was told I could not take all the clothing I brought with us. I was only allowed a few items for each of us at the safe house. Everything else I would have to leave. Can you imagine? More loss! I was steady losing because of my need for love. I keep reiterating this because I want you to understand the root of this dysfunction. I wasn't gaining anything that I thought I needed. Why? Because what I needed wasn't in a man, but in

God. It was in me the whole time, but I couldn't see it, because of the darkness in my life. I allowed the enemy to dim my light and destroy my shine.

I was given a little time to sort through what I thought I needed for all of us. As I sifted through our belongings the tears began to flow again. I felt sick to my stomach, but I had to press through. I wanted to fall out and throw a tantrum, but my babies were watching. After gathering what we would take we were put into another vehicle and driven to the safe house. It was explained to me never to give anyone the location because other people's safety depended on that secrecy. Upon arrival to the building, we were greeted at the door and asked to sit in the waiting area. This was a small room that was either very warm or the stress of everything was catching up with me trying to be strong. A lady came for us and we walked directly into a wash room. We were asked to remove our shoes and socks. The shoes were steamed with a machine and the clothes I brought with us was immediately put into a washer. I was instructed that we would be escorted to our room and plastic bags would be given to me to place our clothes in we were currently wearing.

She said please shower and each of you must wash your hair very well, and someone will be by to pick up your clothing. Not until all of this is done would you be allowed out in general population with the other families. I understand rules and guidelines; however, I was already feeling low and victimized, but having me go through those things made me feel like a victim all over again. I just felt humiliated and imprisoned. I complied of course. A resident assistance aka RA came to get me to go over what was expected of me during my time in the facility. She had to go over the rules, guidelines, and chores. My kids could go to the in-house daycare while I did more paperwork and things were explained. As things were being explained I was told I would be assigned a case worker who had up to 3 days before seeing me. My children would not be allowed to go to daycare until I met with my caseworker. I can remember thinking about my job and how I was going to get fired for not coming to work. At this time, I had been working at my company for ten years. My supervisor was not very understanding either.

As I walked to go get my kids from daycare, I could hear some of the ladies talking amongst themselves about a man and little boy. We went to dinner in the cafeteria and I felt uncomfortable, like everyone was looking at me. I felt embarrassed and ashamed. I didn't have an appetite. My children finished eating and we went back to our room. I could still hear women asking about a man and little boy. I stayed in the room the rest of the day and the next day was September 5th. I took the kids to breakfast and right back into the room. Later, that day I decided it wasn't fair to keep the children locked in a tiny room. We walked upstairs to TV/family room. Once in the TV room the kids began to play and watch TV. One of the other ladies was sitting in the room with us began to talk to me. She asked how I was and if I worked. I said yes, but I no longer have a vehicle to get there. The lady asked what happened to my vehicle. I began to explain my abuser had taken it a couple of days ago. She asked me what kind of vehicle. I explained it was a white four door Chevrolet Tahoe. She looked at me as if she had seen a ghost. I asked what was wrong and she said, "Can I ask you something personal?" I said, yes like what. She asked me the name of my abuser. I slowly looked up at her and our eyes locked. As I began to say Sam, she was saying it at the same time. Her hand immediately covered her mouth in disbelief, shaking her head.

I leaned forward with a confused look on my face. She asked me where my room was. As I began to say downstairs in front of the office, she was saying the same words I was saying. She stood up in shock. I told her that I overheard some ladies asking about a man and little boy. She said yes, Sam was here with your truck and that little boy. As a matter of fact, you are in the same room that he was in. If you would have come a few days earlier, you would of ran into him. I instantly felt sick, nervous and betrayed all at the same time. How could they allow me to stay in the same room knowing what happened to me and that he lived in the same building, not to mention the same room. She then said please don't let the staff know I told you because I could get kicked out, but you should let a RA on duty know he was here. I got up and immediately went downstairs to the office to inform someone. I was talking so fast she didn't understand. I had to explain a few times. For the night and the next morning, I had to stay in that room. The next morning my case worker, a guy named James apologized to me, about my stay. I looked at him saying you knew, he said yes, based on your intake information. He begins to explain they had never had a situation like this and had to figure out where to send me. He in fact had planned for me to go to a shelter in Pasadena because it wasn't safe for me and my kids, but they were full. The staff began to talk about sending me up north and all I could think is what about my job?

The shelter was walking distances to one of our many lab locations. I even reached out to the supervisor of that area asking if I could transfer under her after learning more details of my situation, but she denied me. How was I supposed to take care of my kids? I was doing the best I could with what I had to offer, but it just seemed like I kept getting knocked down on every end. I wasn't catching a break for nothing. I had been beat down to an unbearable level and I didn't have much stamina left. During my time in the shelter this man was still trying to communicate with me through Facebook Messenger. The messages would go from nice, to we need to work this out, to you are nothing and never will be. After all he had done, he still wasn't willing to let go and leave me alone. It felt like I was being antagonized by the enemy. It felt like he wasn't going to give up until I totally gave up and I was just about there, but I was determined to hold on. Our kids depend on us for protection and direction and at that moment I had none of that to offer, but trouble don't last always. A storm will make land fall, tear up some things, flood some cities and even take some lives, but it can't remain a storm forever. Eventually, the sun is going to shine, the water will cease, and the cleanup will begin. This was the only thing I could depend on. I knew in the inner most depths of my heart that a rainbow would form in my life, if I just held on a little while longer. Finally, James loaded me and my kids onto a van and drove us to the next available shelter who was willing to make room for us.

Chapter Seven

"The Bridge Over Troubled Waters"

A bridge is a **_structure_** carrying a road, path, railroad, or canal across a river, ravine, road, railroad, or **_other obstacle._** When I think back to this point of my journey through Domestic Violence, I must acknowledge how good God is. The entire time that I was in my mess, He was not only bridging the gap of the mishaps in my life, but he was building a bridge for me and my kids to cross over, to ensure that we avoid what was lurking in the water. Which brings me to the shelter that James drove us to. Ironically, it was called The Bridge Over Troubled Waters. WOW! No matter how jacked up our lives become, we must know, that we know, that we know, that God ALWAYS has a way of escape prepared for His children. He knew all along what He had in store for me and my babies.

On Friday September 6, 2013, we stood outside waiting on permission to enter the shelter. I had a garbage bag in my right hand with items I got from the previous shelter. My eight-month-old was on my left hip and my two older children were standing in front of me, as we awaited clearance into the shelter. I found myself scoping out my environment and having a self-righteous talk with God. You know those conversations you have when you are in denial about your situation. During my conversation with God, I stressed to Him, how I didn't deserve to be in the position I was in. I kept trying to convince God that I wasn't like the women in the shelter. I didn't deserve to be there. I'm not like these women. I pay my tithes, I go to church, I know I have back slid but I don't deserve this, I shouldn't be here. Well, let me tell you He didn't speak at that moment. When He did speak, He said, take a closer look, you are just like these women. At that moment it felt like a light came on and I was able to see that I was indeed just like those women. I tried to put my bougie self on a pedestal. Today, I understand that I was looking at the situation through my eyes and He saw the total package. These drastic measures were going to serve a greater purpose in my life. Today, I am a living witness of 1st Corinthians 10:13 which says, "God won't put more on you than you can handle."

I had to go through the admittance process all over again of telling my story of how I got there and naming my abuser. I was given a hand book of their rules and process, and we were escorted upstairs to our room. There were daily chores and weekly task. Some of the women had become their abuser. They were treating the other women horrible. I stayed away from that. We lived in the shelter from September 6, 2013 until January 31, 2014. During this time, I spent a lot of nights crying trying to figure out what I had done to end up like this. To be honest at first, I couldn't see what I had done. I was not registering that I played a part in the chaos of my life. I was so busy pointing the finger at my past and what happened to me that I wasn't recognizing that I didn't have to allow the darkness to fuel my life. The word says whatsoever a man sows, that shall he also reap. I was putting some things into the atmosphere that wasn't returning the right kind of harvest. I had to dig deeper into this to ensure that me and my babies would meet a better expected end. For God knew the plans for my life, I just hadn't sought Him to what they were.

In the shelter we were assigned kitchen duty and other daily chores that had to be done. We had to meet with a case worker and attend support group meetings, on top of still trying to work and care for my children. I was trying to keep a sane mind, with no money and no vehicle while trying to figure out how I would get to work. Let's not talk about the pressure of dealing with other battered women, and the whole time I was thinking, "Where is GOD in all of this?" How could He allow this to happen to me? What did I do so bad to cause so much pain to myself and my children? Well, once I stopped tripping, I realized that He was there (GOD) all the time?

One of the hardest things I ever had to do was be totally honest with myself. If I had to use one word to describe it, that would be *accountability*. In order to find myself I had to lose myself by totally surrendering and letting go of everything including my abuser. After being in the shelter a few days, I was called downstairs because I had a visitor. Much to my surprise it was (CPS) Children's Protective Service. The investigator told me she had received a report on me that I was abusive to my children. The investigator interviewed me for about an hour, typing everything I said. She spoke with my two oldest children and checked all three for any signs of physical abuse. After completing her interview, she called her boss to discuss the information I gave her. As I waited to see if she was going to take my kids, I was contemplating in my mind who I could get to take them so they wouldn't end up in the system. I was already in a low place, thinking how I had failed them so much and now this. More devastation. The thought of being separated from them was more than I could handle. After hanging up with her boss I was given a list of things I could and couldn't do.

1. I couldn't have any contact with Sam.

2. I couldn't have my children or myself around Sam.

3. I had to file for a protective order.

4. She as my caseworker could pop in on me at any time.

5. If I moved, I had to notify her ASAP.

6. If I didn't follow any of the rules CPS would take my children.

Wow just like that I had a CPS case. Bad had just gotten worse. When I say the enemy was coming against me like a flood. I felt like I was tossed and driven inside of tsunami. This was on a Monday. On Tuesday I went to work and was able to catch a ride with my oldest children's father. When we pulled into the parking lot, he hit the brakes. I wasn't sure what the problem was, but when I looked up, we both looked at each other in disbelief. My truck was parked at my job. I instantly called the police because I didn't trust him, and I knew what he was capable of. I reached out to my supervisor Ms. T, to inform her that I had to go down to the DA's office. She was telling me that she didn't have coverage for my shift. I stressed the importance, however, I had to wait until that Wednesday. I got there early in the morning and filled out some paperwork. As I waited to be seen my supervisor kept calling to see what time I would be done. I told her I didn't know, but I would be at work as soon as I could. It was taking some time, but I had to get it done. I needed my job, but I couldn't afford to lose my children. Finally, I was called to the back. I was read a statement about reporting false information, then sworn in for my statement. I was escorted into an office to tell my story in reference to what happened to me and my children. I also had to talk about my current CPS case and their orders for me.

The lady pulled up Sam's information and looked over at me saying yeah you had your hands full. She said you are not the first victim, but number four. This is a pattern for him, however, he's smart because he never physically hit you. Threatening you isn't enough to get you a protective order and she told me I was one of the lucky ones. Feeling the way I felt and going through everything I had thus far I didn't feel lucky at all. My whole world had been turned upside down. I started crying and trying to get her to understand that I had to get a protective order to comply with CPS or they would take my children. She asked me to have a seat back in the lobby while she contacted a judge. While sitting in the lobby my supervisor Ms. T started calling again saying she needed me at work now. I started explaining what I was doing and how important getting this done was, but she wouldn't hear of it. I was very upset but decided to leave because I needed my job to take care of my children and myself. On the way to work in Friendswood, the DA's office called and said where are you, I got this approved based on its escalating, his behavior, and the other victims he has done the same thing to before you. She said, I need you to come back and sign your paperwork. I explained that my supervisor needed me at work, so she suggested faxing over a paper to my supervisor requesting I return on the next day. Once I got to work, I faxed that paper to my supervisor. Ms. T called me saying she didn't need the paper that was sent. She said if I needed a day off, I must go through the proper protocol.

I was already feeling the lowest I had ever felt in my life and her I don't care attitude just knocked the breath out of me. I just needed someone to hear me or feel my pain. I just needed a little help. What you see on the surface isn't always what it appears to be. It's not the truth, but a glimpse of what is really going on inside or the hidden weights that we carry. I continued to go to work scared out of my mind constantly looking over my shoulder. I would put a smile on my face and carry on because I still had to work. I spent quite a bit of time sitting at the front desk staring out of the door waiting for him to come and hurt me. After all this is the same guy who stalked me watching for the perfect opportunity to steal my vehicle. I had CPS watching me and scared that he was lurking around. This is a horrible way to live. I was walking on pins and needles every moment of my life. I was thinking about my kids and who would care for them in the event something happened to me. There were so many negative thoughts rambling through my mind over and over again. I spent several restless nights wondering what if?

He continued to call my job. One day I spoke to him and claimed he wanted to give me some money. Sam asked me to come meet him. I began to constantly replay the conversation with the lady at the District Attorney's Office. She said I was one of the lucky ones because I made it out, and whatever I do never agree to meet him anywhere because it was a setup. I reached out to my brother Willie, telling him what Sam wanted me to do. Willie said no. He said whatever you do don't go, as a matter of fact he said give me Sam's number and I will call to setup a meeting with him. I gave Willie, Sam's number, however, he didn't want to meet with Willie. In fact, he gave him some excuse about him not being my legal representative. Imagine that this criminal is talking about something not being legal. Honestly, I didn't expect him to meet with my brother, because men like Sam are afraid to deal with other men. They are weak and will abuse women but are afraid to go up against another man. As sick as this sounds, there are a lot of men in the world who harbor this dysfunction.

Unfortunately, that didn't work so he continued to call my job leaving messages on the voicemail. I can remember leaving for lunch in the white Tahoe. I passed right by Sam and he never saw me because he was so busy trying to get to my job. It really scared me. I felt as if my heart was going to beat out of my chest. I hurried and turned off that road onto Bay Area Blvd. I was so frightened, I pulled into the first parking lot with people walking around so someone could help me or be a witness to what he may do to me. I didn't know what to do so I stood on the sidewalk trembling. I decided enough was enough, I called my Human Resources Department. I began to talk to a lady who's name I can't recall. I said I'm sorry for calling about this, but I need some help, I'm in trouble. I'm being stalked. I started crying and the lady was very patient with me. She told me not to worry she would help me. I explained everything that happened to my kids and myself up to that point. She asked about my supervisor and if I had talked to her and I said yes. I wanted to share how she didn't care and wasn't willing to help, but I didn't. The lady at Human Resources called my supervisor on a conference call. She told my supervisor to reach out to the other supervisor in the area and swap me with one of their employees. She also said she would hire security for the other ladies at the job and to post a picture of him inside our work space facing employees with instructions to call 911 if he came onto the premises.

I was so grateful to this lady at Human Resources. She was great, and I'm sorry I can't remember her name, but the next day I was out of there. I went to work under a supervisor named Nicole who appeared to be heaven sent. She was the only supervisor willing to take me with all my current issues. Nicole was very easy to work for and she didn't ask any questions about my personal issues. She was very open and patient with me. I worked under her for two weeks. I started to relax and feel human again. At the end of that second week my current supervisor Ms. T called, saying it was time for me to come back to my location. I went to Nicole and she told me I was a good employee and she didn't have a problem with me staying at her location. I was so upset about going back to Friendswood and scared. I called Human Resources back and the lady told me it was my supervisors' decision. Needless, to say I went back to Friendswood. The security guard stayed on for one more week. He would escort me to and from my vehicle and stay inside the location all day. The next week on a Tuesday I was on my way to work. I got this sick feeling in my stomach. I knew something wasn't right. Around 10:00am I was standing in the hallway in between servicing patients when I heard my truck crank up.

I ran to the back door and seen my vehicle driving off. I yelled to my coworker to call 911, as I ran back in the building, she told me that she was being told by the 911 operator my truck was being repossessed. I said this isn't a repo. I walked outside to see exactly what was going on. I see a tow truck and a guy hooking my truck up. I walked up to him and asked him what he was doing? He in turn asked who I was. I told him I was the owner of the vehicle and he asked what was my name? He had a strange look on his face, then told me my truck had been turned in by the owner. I said I am the owner and I just paid the truck note. He informed me Sam was the primary on the vehicle and had given that location for a pick up, so he had to take the vehicle. I told him I had items for my kids, and my clothes in the vehicle. He offered to drop the truck, so I could get what I needed but I had nowhere to put those things or even transport them. For crying out loud I was at work! I finally understood God was releasing me from any and everything associated with that domestic violence situation. In the meantime, I paid different people and my kids' father to commute to and from work.

I was stuck between a rock and a hard place. I didn't have very many options, so I reached out to Curtis for advice. The father of my baby daughter worked at a dealership, so I contacted him to explain my situation. He assured me that he could assist me, but after the way he treated me I was reluctant to believe him. I asked Curtis if I should trust him and he said I should, because after proving the baby was his in court, he shouldn't have any reason to mess over me. Well, today I understand that Curtis was saying this from his perspective because he was always there. Unfortunately, Curtis was wrong, and I got played. I should have followed my first mind. My baby daughter's father told me to save up five hundred dollars and he would match it, for a down payment on a new vehicle. I did exactly what he said. I saved up the money and handed it over to him in good faith. Well, he took my money and when confronted, he cursed me out. He told me to stop calling his phone. He stopped taking my phone calls and I was out of five hundred dollars and still without a car. I really had to dig deep for this one. I mean who just purposefully takes advantage of a person when they are down and has no remorse? How do you kick someone when they are already down? This man kicked my legs right from under me and not just me, but my three children, and one being his flesh and blood.

Well, I thank God that He is merciful and that He looks past our faults and sees our needs. I had to completely start over from scratch saving the money to get a vehicle. Determination and perseverance are key elements to having success in life. It wasn't easy, but by Thursday, October 31, 2013, I saved up enough money to get a vehicle. The days of paying people and catching rides were finally over, but it didn't come without a fight. The lesson is…No matter what don't GIVE UP! No matter how bad it looks…don't GIVE UP! No matter how many fiery darts the enemy throws…don't GIVE UP! There is a blessing after the pressing, if you just hold on and not get weary in well doing.

Chapter Eight

"I Finally Found Me"

How can you find something that is lost, especially when you have no idea where to look? My life had become so fragmented that I didn't know where to begin with the Carolyn's life recovery process. I was all over the place and in so many instances I believe that I became numb. Therefore, some of the things I should have been feeling, I wasn't. I completely blocked it out and just started existing. My body was simply going with the daily routines of work, children and watching my back. Honestly, I had left pieces of myself in several places, but I knew that I didn't have the power to recover the pieces, but I knew someone who did. It wasn't going to be easy, but I knew that I had to surrender ALL to God and allow Him to reposition my life. I had lost my self-worth, but when I looked at my babies, I found worth in them, even if I didn't no my own. I knew that I couldn't stop, whether numb or not.

During my time in the shelter, I just happened to encounter more of Sam's drama. One day I was walking into the shelter and his wife was walking out. She had been hiding from him and of course individual cases are not to be discussed, but it somehow still happens because people knew who I was among the staff. Shelter life was very hard! Not only do you have your own issues to sort through, but other women with similar or worse issues. When these issues are not dealt with, the negative communication can become mentally overwhelming. Then we had to deal with the strict rules and chores. Don't get me wrong, I was grateful to have a roof for me and my babies, but it still felt like I was in prison. They truly force you to work hard to get out and not make it a long term crutch.

One Sunday morning I walked to the desk and asked the RA on duty if I could have some washing powder to wash clothes for me and my kids. She said no, claiming that I had come to her the day before to get washing powder. I told her it wasn't me because I was at work. Then she said I had a job and needed to get my own supplies. I stood their feeling horrible, with no money to even purchase washing powder.
I just turned and walked away with tears in my eyes. I couldn't help but think that people hired to work in shelters should undergo a training on how to deal with the women in the shelter. What is wrong with being a little sensitive to woman who are in distress, especially if you are a woman? However, this was not my first time encountering this RA.

I started washing my clothes at night because I could get it done faster without interruption. It was close to changing shifts and the RA who always seem to give everyone a hard time was coming on duty. My clothes were not finished drying so before shift change, I asked permission to allow extra time for our clothes to finish drying and the RA's on duty said yes it was fine. However, shift changed and this RA that seemed to always give everyone a hard time came on duty. She took my clothes out of the dryer and took them to the office without me knowing. So, as I go to check on my clothes they were gone. I went to the desk to ask if she knew what happened to my clothes. She told me how she is going to write me up for going pass the allotted time in the washing area. She also said because I did that, she had to drag my, wet clothes to the office and how she didn't appreciate having to do that. I tried to explain I got permission, however she wouldn't hear it, rudely cutting me off.

I also remember having issues with one of the ladies, who was hating on me because I lived in the shelter, but I had a job. What she didn't understand was my issue wasn't working, it was safety. This lady called CPS on me and a detective was sent out because it was reported I abused my kids. I tell you the enemy is always lurking, and he has workers in place everywhere. This meant I not only had one CPS case, but now two. He was trying to break me. I refused! I might have bent a lot, but I wasn't going to break. Thankfully, the detective came out, introduced himself and then talked and played with my babies. He determined that this was a fraudulent report. He asked if I knew who or why and I explained to him some of the women were jealous and felt like I didn't belong in the shelter because I had a job and a vehicle. How many of you know God will take a mess and use it to bless you? After determining that my kids were fine the detective explained that during the holidays his department picked families that needed help. He asked if it would be alright to add my children and myself to that list. I said of course it would. The detective took my name and the children's names and ages. Days before Christmas the officer called me asking if I could meet him down the street. When I arrived to meet the officer, he filled my car up with everything you could possibly think of. My Father was showing me His mighty right hand in the midst of my situation. I must interject this small nugget of wisdom. If you have found yourself in a situation similar to mine, keep your eyes on God. Yes, the fleshly part of you and your soul will ache, but weeping only endures for a night, but joy will come in the morning. Please note it didn't say what morning, it just said in the morning. This means you must be steadfast and unmovable until that time comes. With all that I encountered I could have easily thrown in the towel and felt justified by it, but GOD! Joseph told his brothers after they threw him in the pit and sold him into slavery, he told them what you meant for evil, God used it for my good. This was the same situation. All that Sam, the RA, the hating lady and everyone else who wronged me, including myself, was going to work out for my good. After the officer loaded up my vehicle, I thanked him and drove away. I was so grateful. I'm still grateful because this brought me hope and boosted my faith in God. After six months of dealing with CPS my case was dismissed.

During my time in the shelter I had weekly chores that had to be done at night, but I couldn't take my kids. So, I would wait for them to fall asleep to go do the chores. Once I was done, I would come back to the room and cry my eyes out up at 5:00am. I would clean the room in preparation to leave by 6:00am to get to work like nothing is wrong. I can remember having a patient come in during the Christmas holiday for me to draw her blood. We carried on the normal conversation. I had been drawing her blood for years and she had seen me through each one of my pregnancies. I finished her up and hurried to the shelter because it had been announced we had a mandatory meeting happening and everyone had to be there. I got my kids and went down to the cafeteria. It was set up with different vendors and a very nice dinner had been brought in for us. As I gathered my three kids in line to receive dinner, I looked up and locked eyes with my patient whose blood I had just drawn. I could feel the tears coming in my eyes as she looked at me. She whispered Carolyn are you ok? I managed to shake my head fighting to keep from crying. As we approached her serving area, she started talking to my kids calling each one of their names and introducing herself. We moved along in the line to finish dinner and the activities. We didn't really say anything else that night. However, she was a monthly blood draw, so I knew she was coming into the lab to get her blood drawn. On the date of her next visit, I called her to the back and as soon as the door closed, she gave me the biggest hug. She started apologizing to me saying how sorry she was and if I was ok or if there was anything she could do to help. It just goes to show how people can be and are in all types of situations. Some you may know and some you have no idea of or will never know. When I saw my patient, I didn't know if I was more hurt or embarrassed. Even though I found myself in a situation I couldn't control, no one wants to live an unstable life. Situations, circumstances and unhealthy decisions thrust us into places that are not always pretty. Yet, through the grace of God, I stand today to tell my story of endurance, empowerment and overcoming to encourage someone else. When I think back over what could have happened. When I think about the number of women who didn't make it or those who are currently in shelters or being attacked, I rejoice because I know that God raised me up to be a Voice for the domestically voiceless. You don't have to be a victim, I know that it appears there is no way out, but God said He will provide a way of escape. The tricky thing about this is, we don't know the day or the time, we must believe that He will.

God is always working and moving through your pain, which ties in with your purpose. Sometimes the slightest gestures or comments can put you back into your abusive situation. Which in my opinion means that total deliverance hasn't taken place? This means you are still operating in survivorship mode and there is still much work to be done. Survivorship mood is still fighting for what doesn't belong or fits any longer. Coming out of a survivorship mode means letting your guards down and going into thriving mode. What does thriving mode look like after surviving? I'm glad you asked. It means your guards are down and you are making efforts towards a positive direction because it all works together. I can tell you many reasons why to leave an unhealthy abusive relationship, but it will not happen or take place until you know your worth and the value God has bestowed upon you. Wake up my sisters for you are worth more than gold. Stand up and take your life back. Take your joy back. Take your peace back. Take your dignity and self-esteem back. This is the season of the take-back. Even if you have to stand in the mirror and talk to yourself. This doesn't make you crazy, because the word says, David encouraged himself in the Lord. Sometimes drastic situations call for drastic measures.

After being in the shelter for quite some time, me and my babies were finally transitioning to a new place. The shelter owned an apartment complex named Destiny Village. I met each of the requirements for me to move into a unit. We lived there from January 2014 until March 2015.

This was the time that I allowed God to fully purge my heart and heal me of my brokenness. After allowing God to complete the work in me, I went to the apartment office in February to thank them for the opportunity and all the help that was provided. I told them that I was ready to be released and move on. It was time for another woman waiting in the shelter to occupy that space. I was not afraid anymore and began to use my voice to tell my story. As I began telling my story, I started getting my power back. Women were being blessed and set free when I opened my mouth, therefore, I learned that there is power in our words and what we speak. Revelation 3:11 says, "We overcome by the blood of the lamb, and by the words of our testimony." I was an overcomer! During the battle I didn't see a way out, but God did. My hope in telling my true story is that this book will help other women or men realize and understand the dysfunction and destruction of remaining or entering an abusive relationship. Please get out while you are still breathing, or before any hurt or harm comes to you or your children. Pay attention to the warning signs and always let someone know if you have been or feel threatened. This is my prayer for you!

BE A VOICE NOT A VICTIM!

Ladies Overcoming Fear Together (LOFT) was birth out of my experience with domestic violence. A situation I was desperately needing to escape. In the beginning I was blinded to abusive behavior because it wasn't physical. I learned the hard way that abuse comes in many forms. This lesson of abuse would cost me a great deal. I found myself suffering financial, economic, verbal, psychological and emotional abuse. Having the will power to overcome these various forms of abuse caused me to become impregnated with purpose. A purpose greater than myself, that open the door for me to snatch abused people out of the grips of the enemy and their abuser, by simply being a voice.

Let me break down and define the various forms of abuse because I want to make sure it is comprehensible.

Financial abuse is defined as illegal or unauthorized use of a person's property.

Economic abuse is defined as when one intimate partner has control over the other partner's access.

Verbal abuse is defined as a negative defining statement told about the victim or directly to the victim.

Psychological abuse is defined or characterized by a person subjecting or exposing another person to behavior that may result in psychological trauma, including anxiety, chronic depression, or post- traumatic stress disorder.

Emotional abuse is defined as an attempt to control; the perpetrator of emotional abuse uses emotion as his/her weapon of choice.

These are self-explanatory, but we can see ourselves in this situation, but have no clue how to get out. Even after experiencing all these things I could not find the strength or courage to leave, as you read in previous chapters. It wasn't that I didn't know I needed to leave, I was afraid to leave. I was emotionally, mentally, psychologically and physically paralyzed. I was literally being tormented, because fear brings torment. I couldn't stop thinking of the what if's or trying to think two steps ahead of my abuser and it was exhausting. I convinced myself that I couldn't make it on my own, especially once I started having children. I lost myself and my freedom to the abuser. It felt like I was hypnotized and under a spell that couldn't be broken. People would ask me why I stayed and why I kept going back and my lamebrain excuse was because I loved him. Well, truth be told I didn't love myself, and he didn't love me, because he didn't love himself. Do you see the unhealthy cycle of abuse we were both subjected to? He was sick and so was I. See in order to heal and move forward, YOU MUST BE HONEST! To overcome you must be willing to overlook the person, release the pain to God and move forward.

Overcoming means to press forward; keep pushing; to prevail over your weakness. My weakness was making sound decisions because I was forced to learn how to do this amid all the bad ones I had already made. My driving force were my babies. It is imperative that you know what you are fighting for. If you don't have anything to fight for, then nine times out of ten, it will be much easier to give up. I can recall days and weeks at a time where I rehearsed the speech about getting out of my situation. Well, that was all I was doing, was talking with no actions. Every time I even thought I had a plan, he would sucker me right back in and me with my low self-esteem would get reeled right back in. I knew within the depths of my soul that I wasn't my own person anymore. What I hadn't concluded was the time that it truly started. Was it at the age of four when I was molested or with the first guy, the second guy, the third guy or maybe it was a result of it all? Who really knows? What I did know was that I had to change how I responded to my situation. I could no longer make rash decisions based on my emotions and expect positive results. This might work for some people, but it wasn't working for me. I was being controlled his suggestive thoughts and comments, that eventually drowned out my own thoughts. I found myself acting out or reacting based on his suggestions, without realizing he was controlling my every move, even with my children.

With that being said, LOFT is an organization designed by a formerly abused woman who is now healed, for women who have been or currently is being abused. I didn't have anywhere to turn or people who understood what I was going through WITHOUT JUDGEMENT. That is the key when encountering an abusive relationship, you are already embarrassed and then to have people judge you makes you remain silent. We are breaking through silence through LOFT and becoming proactive voices that impact the world one man, woman, boy and girl at a time.

LOFT Inspirational Treasures

I. Don't Be A Victim, Be a Voice!

When an individual becomes a victim to any form of abuse, the first thing they lose is their voice. They either become silent on their own, or they are forced into silence by the violator. Silence causes you to internalize your thoughts, feeling and emotions, which can become very unhealthy. Therefore, we must be willing to let our thoughts be heard. We must find our voice that has been put on mute because of how insignificant you've been made to feel. Use your voice to express your thoughts and ideas reaching out to other women who are enduring or have endured domestic violence. It occurs more often than we know in schools, homes, work places, even in church. It's not always physical as I grew up thinking throughout my lifetime but emotional, verbal, economic mental, financial, sexual, and cultural abuse. Talk to someone you'd be surprised at how many other women have experienced or still currently deal with abusive relationships for various reasons. We spend so much time expecting loyalty from someone who can't even be honest with themselves recognizing they have an issue or problem that need to be attended to before having a relationship with anyone. We must realize when we are being lied to and when we are lying to ourselves. Once we recognize we have been lied to there is a choice to make either we breathe life into that lie by believing it and helping it grow through our support of repeating or clinging on to it however there is another choice we stop it dead in its tracks. The choice is yours; how will you decide?

II.   I Am My Sister's Keeper

A *keeper* is a person who manages or looks after something or someone. In this life we experience many challenges and most people chose to deal with life on their own. Yet, when it comes to issues such as domestic violence, we should always be willing to lend an ear, a hand, a hug, and an open heart. We must understand that every situation is different and just because we fall short in our choices doesn't mean we don't need help. It could simply mean we lost our way and just need someone else to help us find it. It is very easy to get in a delusion or fairy tale that we have created in our minds, that can lead us off on a destructive path. A path that most times, takes someone else to come along and help get back on the right path. Sometimes all it takes is a kind word, someone to say it will be ok and you will make it. Someone to say don't give up hope and offer sound, not judgmental advice. Then on the other hand it also takes someone who is willing to get in our faces in love and give us the hardcore truth. Someone who is willing to tell us we are tripping and its time to think about self and let the foolishness go. That someone who will encourage us to see our true value and worth, then tell us to rise ABOVE our present circumstances. That sister who is willing to be quick to listen and slow to speak.

Truth be told, most of the times we know what needs to be done, but we're either not ready or strong enough to make a move. It takes more strength to leave than stay. As women we desire to have that fairy tale relationship that we read about as little girls. We look for that knight in shining armor. He can very well show up as a knight, but then turn into a monster. Many times, the monster doesn't reveal themselves until our emotions and feelings are in too deep. The harsh reality is some men are hurting and need healing themselves.

Hurt people, hurt people which means they have no filter when it comes to lashing out, inflicting pain, and wreaking havoc on unsuspecting individuals. However, it's not our job to fix their brokenness by becoming life size targets or punching bags.

Therefore, it is imperative that we be alert and watchful when it comes to other women. Many times, abused women will be introverted and isolated, but we need to be willing to ask questions. We must be willing to be bold and to let our sisters know we are praying for them and will help them if needed. It makes a difference when you are in an abusive situation and you KNOW that you have a way of escape if needed. Most women don't leave abusive situations because they don't have anywhere to go, especially if they have children.

III. Smiling Through the Tears

I'm sure you've heard the cliché "Fake it till you make it" several times over the course of your life. Well, I must concur that it works, but it is very deceptive. I spent a lot of time and years walking around with a fake smile plastered on my face, while I was bleeding out my heart. The pain ran deep. It was hurt on top of hurt. I was completely numb, and I walked around in a daze with my head held down. My confidence and self-esteem were low. I couldn't look people in their faces when I was speaking to or with them, or as they were talking to me. I didn't feel worthy. I was lost. I would put on a fake smile to keep going. Then at night when the lights were out, and my kids were sleeping, and I was all alone.; the real and true Carolyn came out. All the hurt from being a messed-up girl, who grew into a broken woman; which made it easy to be manipulated and coerced into abusive narcissistic relationships. All because I didn't know my worth or value and the cycle continued until I found myself in the fight of my life, for my freedom and the freedom of my children. Don't get me wrong you have to do what works for you, but whatever you do, don't stay stuck in the same rut. Smile through the pain, while you are devising a plan to do better and be better. Smile through the pain, knowing that eventually the smile is going to manifest the true intended results of a happy life, without abuse. You never let the abuser know they are getting the best of you. Kill them with kindness and let your heavenly Father do the rest. Vengeance belongs to Him and only Him.

IV. Transformation

When something or someone is *transformed*, there is a thorough or dramatic change in form, appearance or the character of. I can honestly say today, that I experienced several transformations throughout my life. Some were good and some not so good, but through it all I persevered and have overcome. The greatest transformation in my life took place when I finally realized that I couldn't continue to allow my feelings and emotions to dictate my life. You see, as you read each chapter, you witness a life that was run on emotions and feelings. I arrived at the drastic conclusion of insanity when I found myself at ground zero. It took me losing everything to realize I was following the same dysfunctional patterns but expecting a different result. This was never going to manifest because I was operating out of my broken place. Broken + broken= More brokenness! Oh, but the day finally came, when I said enough is enough and I made the choice to look inward first and to deal with Carolyn and her demons from the past. I took back my power from the grips of the enemy and set my focus on God, then myself and then my children. When I did this not only did my outside appearance have a dramatic change, but inside as well. I found forgiveness, peace, joy, happiness, and love. I forgave those who wronged me, but most importantly I forgave myself for allowing it. This caused wholeness to manifest in my life. I was able to find true love and trust from and through God. When I allowed Carolyn to get out of the way, allowing God to order my steps, He sent my husband Wendell Hunter. Yes, I is married yall! I let go of the past and allowed healing to manifest by releasing everything that was designed to hinder and kill me. It was only by the grace of God that I didn't lose my life. It was only the grace of God that I didn't lose my children or even I could have snapped and hurt the abuser. There are so many ways that my ending could have played out, but God saw fit for me to overcome to that I could be a voice for other victims. So that I could show others what it looks like to be abused and not even see the damage being done. This is my true story of survival, determination, overcoming, that finally led to sheer happiness. Please be advised that everything in life has a process. Getting into a relationship is easy, the process of getting out, if needed, can be difficult and tedious. If you don't know who you are or what your purpose, take some time for self-reflection. This will guarantee that you choose the right person for your life. Learn to love and date you. Learn to love God and spend quality time with Him. In due time you will REAP, if you do not faint. The TRANSFORMATION is great when you do it with the Lord.

BE A VOICE NOT A VICTIM!

Final Words

"Gratitude, Encouragement & Grace"

I would like to express my deepest gratitude for reading "From a Victim to a Voice" and I pray that you were blessed by the transparency of my testimony. Taking a long hard look at my journey is the first step towards investing in yourself. You must arrive at the place of self-reflection, where you seek to understand that you may be tolerating something that can cause you great discomfort and even death. In dealing with domestic violence it is imperative that you learn yourself and learn the person you are dealing with. We must grow up and not be so easily tossed and driven. We must foster positive thinking and remember your perspective becomes your reality. Drop the weights and remember wisdom comes in time. I myself started as a mess based on someone else's demons and dysfunctions, but God turned my mess into a message. He has used my dysfunction and shame to create a diamond that was formed through great hardship. I am a living, breathing, walking miracle. I have learned to listen with my heart and spirit, not my ears. I have learned to set healthy boundaries. Everything requires work and I had to learn to separate the issues from the problems and then separate the person from the problem. I myself suffered wrong for right by admitting, quitting, and forgetting to move on. To live a peaceful life, you must be willing to do the behind the scenes work. Work that only you and God can participate in, such as forgiveness, re-learning your value and self-worth, and learning how to live with someone until total healing has manifested. You must learn how to stop the cycle. Walk away! Walk away empowered, different from the way you walked in. Be open to what is possible. Reflect on what you've been thinking and dreaming about? Take the first step to identify your WOW factor. Your WOW factor helps you to determine your value to self and then to others. We have been called to live a life of freedom in Christ. We were not created to be slaves and abused. If you are in an abusive situation…RUN for YOUR LIFE! Be cautious in your efforts but choose life and CHOOSE YOU! You will be glad you did! Once you get out, get healed and get right…Amplify Your Voice for others who need to get out before its too late.

Author Bio

Evangelist Carolyn Hunter

Carolyn works professionally as a trained, phlebotomists to help improve and touch people lives one touch at a time. Her passion has always been helping others in any aspect applicable for her. In early 2013 Carolyn experienced a major setback and lived to tell her story about enduring domestic violence at the hands of her abuser. After escaping in the middle of the night seeking shelter and hiding, she found herself, rebuilding her life from scratch. Living in a battered woman shelter, later moving into a transitional housing program. Living with those ladies daily allowed Carolyn to see there was something on a much larger scale needed. It was through her experience and time spent in and around the shelter LOFT was birthed. Ladies Overcoming Fear Together a nonprofit organization came from a very painful time in Carolyn's life however her purpose was greater than her pain now God has released her to tell her story of overcoming in the hopes of inspiring someone else "Don't be a Victim be a Voice," as a wife, mother, public speaker Carolyn understands the struggle of everyday life. LOFT is an organization that is spreading and heighten awareness about domestic violence.

Have you ever fell victim to anything, it could have been a person, place or thing? If you answered yes, I must say you're not alone myself included. In life we move fast and want things to happen right away however we must trust the process it takes. Let's take this journey together learning how to overcome fear and use our voices. I would like to introduce myself my name is Carolyn Hunter and I am a survivor of domestic violence. My purpose is to educate and spread awareness in the hope of helping and even preventing others male and female alike from enduring such harsh matters. Violence doesn't discriminate rich, poor, young, old, race or sex, however awareness is the key.

Contact Information

Email: ladiesoft@gmail.com

Email: carolyn@ladiesoft.org

Website: ladiesoft.org

Facebook: @LadiesOvercomingFearTogether

Radio Broadcast: Raise the Praise 100 Houston
www.raisethepraise100.com
Couples Corner
Saturdays 1pm to 4pm

BE A VOICE NOT A VICTIM!

Made in the USA
Middletown, DE
17 March 2019